Tank Warfare

Below: Matilda squadron of 4 RTR advancing in staggered line-ahead, adopted to avoid the dust of the tank in front. (IWM)

COMBAT DEVELOPMENT IN WORLD WAR TWO

Tank Warfare

Bryan Perrett

ARMS AND
ARMOUR

Other books by Bryan Perrett:

Tank Tracks to Rangoon
The Czar's British Squadron
Weapons of the Falklands Conflict
A History of Blitzkrieg
Knights of the Black Cross – Hitler's Panzerwaffe and its Leaders
Soviet Armour since 1945
Desert Warfare
Jungle Warfare

First published in Great Britain in 1990 by Arms and Armour Press, Artillery House, Artillery Row, London SW1P 1RT.

Distributed in the USA by Sterling Publishing Co. Inc., 387 Park Avenue South, New York, NY 10016-8810.

Distributed in Australia by Capricorn Link (Australia) Pty. Ltd, P.O. Box 665, Lane Cove, New South Wales 2066, Australia.

British Library Cataloguing in Publication Data
Perrett, Bryan *1934 –*
Tank Warfare.
1. Armoured combat vehicles: Tanks, history
I. Title   II. Series
623.74'752'09
ISBN 0-85368-993-8

Designed and edited by DAG Publications Ltd. Designed by David Gibbons; edited by Michael Boxall; layout by Anthony A. Evans; typeset by Ronset Typesetters Ltd, Darwen, Lancs; line illustrations by Sampleskill Ltd and by Chris Westhorp; camerawork by M&E Reproductions, North Fambridge, Essex; printed and bound in Great Britain by The Bath Press, Avon.

Below: Stuarts belonging to the reconnaissance troop of a British armoured regiment seen during the breakout from the Normandy beachhead.

Contents

Introduction: The Anatomy of the Tank

The name 'tank' is actually an historical accident arising from the need to conceal the true purpose of these vehicles while they were in their embryonic development stage. In the United Kingdom the first tanks were built by William Foster and Co. Ltd. of Lincoln under the cover story that they were mobile water cisterns, i.e., tanks, for use on the Eastern Front, and a photograph exists showing one in the factory yard clearly inscribed in Cyrillic characters 'With Care to Petrograd'. The name stuck and, just as we often inaccurately refer to a raincoat as a Mackintosh or to a vacuum cleaner as a Hoover, the most powerful family of armoured fighting vehicles (AFVs) has been called tanks by most of the world ever since. The French, who were just behind the British in producing tanks, called them *chars d'assault* (assault vehicles).

Strictly speaking, the large rhomboidal British tanks of the First World War and their French contemporaries, the Schneider and Saint Chamond, were assault guns rather than tanks, since their main armament was housed in limited traverse mountings. The first true tank, that is an AFV with its major weapon system housed in a turret capable of all-round traverse, was the French 6.5-ton Renault FT-17, armed with a short 37mm gun or a single machine-gun. This was protected by 22mm armour, had a maximum speed of 5mph and was manned by a crew of two. The vehicle was introduced in 1917 and by the time the Armistice had been concluded more than 3,000 had been built; many were still serving in 1940 and a few were encountered in 1942 during the Anglo-American landings in French North Africa.

The primary purpose of the tank is to use its mobility and the protection provided by its armour to bring its gun within killing range of the enemy. The advantage of a turret with all-round traverse therefore requires little emphasis and once this was a reality it determined the basic layout of the tank, which has remained essentially unaltered to this day. This layout consists of a forward driving compartment containing the driver and his controls, a fighting compartment housing the turret crew and gun control equipment, and an engine compartment at the rear containing the vehicle's power unit and fuel tanks.

Before proceeding further, however, it is necessary to examine the basic anatomy of the tank if the technical developments which took place prior to and during the

Below: A preserved Tank Mk V taking part in the parade held to commemorate the Royal Tank Regiment's 50th birthday. The Chinese eye is a distinction retained by 4 RTR. The first British and French tanks were really assault guns.

Second World War are to be related correctly to their operational context. In the years immediately following the Great War there was a tendency in some circles to regard the machine-gun as the tank's principal armament. It was soon realized that on the battlefield tank could hardly avoid meeting tank, and for this sort of encounter the machine-gun was almost useless. There was, therefore, an immediate need to arm tanks with a gun that was capable of defeating the opponents' armour. Thus, the choice of a gun with the ability to penetrate the thickest armour currently in service became the starting-point of every major tank design.

In this respect the critical factor was the diameter of the turret ring, which had to be wide enough not only to absorb the weapon's full recoil, but also permit the loader to handle his ammunition quickly and efficiently; if designers were wise, sufficient spare capacity was left within the diameter to allow up-gunning, i.e., fitting a larger weapon, should the need arise. It will, therefore, be immediately apparent that the size of the turret ring also determined the width of the tank's hull into which it was set. This, in turn, set designers a further problem, namely the need to contain the overall dimensions of the vehicle; during the inter-war years, for example, British designers were inhibited by the need to conform to the limitations of the standard railway loading gauge, while their German counterparts were restricted by a 24-ton bridge-loading specification. The tank's secondary armament, consisting of one or more machine-guns, presented no such difficulties. Normally, one machine-gun was mounted coaxially with the main armament, while a second was housed in the front plate of the hull, where it was operated by the co-driver.

The main and coaxial armament mountings were protected by a slab of thicker armour known as a mantlet, lying across the turret front. Within the turret the

gun control equipment consisted of traverse and elevation handwheels, which operated on corresponding toothed rings, the telescopic gunsight and firing triggers. Ammunition was stowed in ready-use racks or bins within easy reach of the loader, with additional supplies under the turret floor. British and German practice required three-man turret crews in which the vehicle commander sat at the rear and to one side of the turret with the gunner and his gun control equipment immediately in front and below, and the loader across the gun on the opposite side of the turret. In British crews the loader also operated the radio set, which was located in a bustle at the rear of the turret; American, French and German tank radios, however, were located in the hull and usually operated by the co-driver.

Having selected their primary weapon system and decided how their tank was to be fought, the designers' next step would be to choose a suitable power unit. They would already be aware of the vehicle's dimensions and the type and thickness of armour to be employed, so it was a simple matter to calculate the weight that had to be moved and the degree of power needed to produce the speed demanded by its users. The higher the power to weight ratio, the greater would be the vehicle's mobility. Rather less simple were the problems of fitting the engine together with its air and liquid cooling systems, fuel and lubricant tanks, into the confined space available. Simultaneously, the users would specify performance requirements which were seldom compatible with the machinery, including low fuel consumption, the ability to operate in heavy dust and extremes of temperature, the capacity to run for long periods without attention, and accessibility for ease of maintenance. Inevitably, compromises had to be made. On the other hand, during the 1920s and 1930s great strides were made in automotive technology and these offered designers a wide variety of alternative engine choice including petrol or diesel, liquid- or air-cooled, in-line, Vee, rotary or horizontally opposed. A number of these had been developed for use in aircraft and others for use in commercial vehicles; the latter were obviously smaller and were sometimes used in pairs or larger combinations.

Below: The French Renault FT of 1917, fitted with a traversing turret, was the first recognizable ancestor of the modern tank. (RAC Tank Museum)

Perhaps the most notable tank engine of the period was the Russian lightweight water-cooled V-12 diesel, producing 500hp at 1,800rpm, which was fitted to the T-34 and KV Series, giving excellent service throughout the war and for many years after. The rotary aircraft engines used in some American tank designs were both reliable and powerful, but their height was a major disadvantage resulting in a tall vehicle silhouette and a degree of internal inconvenience caused by the high drive shaft. Conversely, the Churchill owed its comparatively low silhouette to its 'flat' Bedford Twin Six 350hp horizontally opposed petrol engine. For their part, the Japanese developed air-cooled diesel tank engines which were ideal for use in tropical climates, although this was to be their major contribution to tank technology. The choice of petrol or diesel fuel was made by armies on the basis of what would be most readily available in wartime, the general – but far from invariable – rule being that the Americans, British, French and Germans preferred petrol, while the Italians, Japanese and Russians used diesel.

From the engine the line of drive passed through the gearbox to the drive sprockets, which drove the tracks. The designers had to decide whether they wished their vehicle to have front or rear drive sprockets, there being advantages and disadvantages to be had with both. Front drive sprockets mean shorter gearbox and steering linkages, but the transmission components absorb vital space within the fighting and driving compartments. Rear drive sprockets shorten the line of drive, leave the fighting and driving compartments unencumbered, but accumulate compacted earth and debris to the point at which they will throw a track.

Most gearboxes of the period were of the manually operated 'crash' or synchromesh type, the former requiring the driver to double de-clutch, although some pre-selector boxes were in use. Whatever system was employed the tank's tracks acted as a brake during the pause between gear changes, so that the driver was unable to take advantage of the vehicle's momentum as he would if he were driving a wheeled vehicle. This factor was known as rolling resistance and to compensate the driver used his engine revolution counter to produce the appropriate engine speed for the required gear.

In the majority of cases tanks were steered by clutch-and-brake mechanisms. To turn right, for example, the driver pulled back on his right steering lever, separating and braking the line of drive to the right drive sprocket, the effect of this being to stop the right track while the left track continued to revolve. The system wasted a great deal of power and as tanks became heavier steering brakes tended to overheat quickly. Much effort was directed into producing regenerative steering systems in which, by means of gears, one track was slowed down rather than braked while the other was speeded up. This line of research led towards the incorporation of gearbox, differential and steering mechanisms into a single unit, the most significant development being the Merritt-Maybach gearbox of 1938, versions of which were employed in the British Churchill and German Tiger E tanks.

The tank's running gear consisted of its suspension, drive sprockets, idler wheels, top return rollers, roadwheels and tracks. There were many types of suspension, and designers would choose a system that provided the crew with the smoothest possible ride as well as giving a steady gun platform if firing on the move were contemplated. Coil springs attached to pivoting bogie wheels were commonly used, as were leaf springs. The torsion bar suspension, in which roadwheels are suspended individually from trailing arms attached to under-floor tension-sprung transverse bars, was introduced by the Germans in 1936 and widely adopted. A high-speed cross-country suspension was invented by the American engineer J. Walter Christie, consisting of large diameter roadwheels individually hung from cranks which were cushioned by vertical coil springs housed within the hull; this was adopted by the Russians for their BT (Fast Tank) Series of the 1930s and was also used in the majority of British Cruiser Tank designs.

Tracks were initially made from hardened cast iron but these did not wear well and were replaced by manganese steel tracks which had a much longer life. The Americans developed tracks from rubber blocks linked by external end pieces. After some use all tracks stretch and it becomes necessary to restore their tension by adjusting the position of the idler wheel; when no more adjustment is possible one or more links can be removed.

During the inter-war years the tank's armour was arranged in a simple box-like format which presented a series of flat surfaces to the enemy's fire, the reason being that designers had yet to appreciate that angled armour provided better ballistic protection. If, for example, an armoured plate 45mm thick is laid back at an angle of 60 degrees, the horizontal distance which the enemy round has to penetrate is actually 90mm. The first application of this principle was made by the Russians with their 1937 A-20 design, which led in due course to their renowned T-34 medium tank. Again, for the first part of this period, tank armour tended to be of uniform thickness all round and it was only in the mid-1930s that heavier frontal armour began to the fitted, this being the area against which most of the enemy's fire would obviously be directed.

Advances in metallurgical technology resulted in the adoption of various types of armour with outer and inner layers of differing Brinell hardness, but the introduction of homogeneous (uniform hardness) nickel-chrome-molybdenum steel armour proved to be a major step forward. 'Hard' homogeneous armour had a Brinell factor of 450 and could not be machined; 'soft' homogeneous armour, on

Below: Vickers Medium Tanks of the Experimental Mechanized Force on Salisbury Plain. (RAC Tank Museum)

the other hand, had a factor of 380 and could be worked after heat treatment. The Germans preferred to use face-hardened rolled plate, which offered high resistance to solid armour-piercing shot. For much of the period armour plates were bolted or riveted together, a major disadvantage of this method being that the force of a projectile striking a bolt or rivet head was transferred to the inner fastening, which could sheer and fly round the vehicle's interior with the velocity of a bullet. Joint welding was introduced by the Germans and Russians in the middle 1930s, simultaneously solving this problem, reducing weight and increasing production, the British and Americans following suit some years later. Cast armour has slightly inferior ballistic qualities to those of rolled plate and for this reason has to be correspondingly thicker, but it does lend itself to

the manufacture of difficult shapes with differing internal and external curvatures, for example turrets and bow pieces. The French fitted a cast turret to their D-1 tank of 1931 and although other nations were slow to adopt the idea, it was firmly if not universally established by the outbreak of the Second World War. Designers were also required to provide protection against the phenomenon known as bullet splash, which had been encountered by tank and armoured car crews during the First World War. Spurts of molten lead from small-arms ammunition penetrating visors, hatch openings and joints in the armour could blind a crewman, or inflict minor but extremely painful wounds. By 1939 much had been done to eliminate the problem by improved jointing, better hatch seatings, bullet-proof vision blocks and episcopes, but it was not completely eradicated.

1. Tank Technology of the Second World War

THE STATE OF THE ART IN 1939

The correct application of new technology to future wars is one of the more difficult aspects of generalship. The tank had been called into being in a situation in which the powers of defence in the form of machine-guns, concentrated artillery and barbed wire were greater than those of an attacking force, and it had succeeded in restoring mobility to the battlefield. The question facing senior officers in the years following 1918, therefore, was how tanks were to be employed in the next major conflict, and on this subject there were wide differences of opinion.

Some senior officers, in fact, took the view that the tank had a very limited future. One suggestion was that since the tank had broken the trench deadlock, similar deadlocks were unlikely to occur again and if they did they could be dealt with by other means. This, of course, was wishful thinking at its most negative. Another was that the development of anti-tank guns was in itself tantamount to passing a death sentence on the tank, ignoring the fact that the inevitable reaction of designers would be to protect their product with thicker armour.

The majority, however, took the sensible view that technology could not be un-learned and that the tank was here to stay. The most dramatic theories concerning its future use were those put forward by the then Colonel J. F. C. Fuller in his Plan 1919, which envisaged a holding operation to tie down the main body of the enemy's army while a deep penetration force of tanks and lorried infantry, supported by aircraft,

destroyed his higher headquarters; this, Fuller reasoned, would result in the strategic paralysis of the opposing force which, lacking direction from above, would disintegrate under sustained pressure. Fuller's concept, and indeed the whole idea of self-contained armoured formations, was welcomed by the more progressive military theorists, notably Captain Basil Liddell Hart, the military correspondent of the *Daily Telegraph*.

There were, of course, no precedents for such ideas and no means of telling whether they would work. General Staffs, therefore, were reluctant to commit themselves to so radical an approach without first being convinced of its validity. In the meantime, they were fully aware that the tank also had more traditional applications. Of these, support for infantry operations was the most obvious, but since it was also generally accepted that horsed cavalry had had its day, tanks would additionally be required to perform the customary cavalry roles of reconnaissance, pursuit and exploitation. This led to a frequently heated debate in which the progressive elements argued that such diversions failed to realize the tank's true potential, but the truth was that the infantry could hardly be denied armoured support and the cavalry simply could not function without AFVs. The British and French armies also required tanks to perform the role of imperial policing in their vast overseas territories.

The fact was that no one knew quite what to expect and every major army sought to cover all possible contingencies by building a far wider variety of tanks than was strictly necessary. These ranged from heavy breakthrough tanks through two classes of infantry tank to medium or cruiser tanks, light tanks and turretless tankettes, the last being little more than tracked machine-gun carriers. In 1939 the doctrines governing their deployment and the organization of the formations in which they served differed extensively from country to country.

UNITED KINGDOM

Thanks to the deliberate political neglect of all its armed services, the United Kingdom's contribution to the science of armoured warfare during the inter-war years was largely intellectual. The Tank Corps, which in November 1918 had consisted of 25 battalions, had been reduced to five battalions and twelve

armoured car companies by 1921, one battalion being permanently assigned to man the Corps' depot at Bovington. There was a real possibility that it might have been disbanded altogether had it not been for the personal interest shown by its Colonel-in-Chief, His Majesty King George V, who in 1923 granted it the title Royal and ensured its permanent place on the Army List. Simultaneously, Liddell Hart, now firmly convinced that the tank offered a means of winning wars without enormous loss of life, produced a stream of articles and books which brought Fuller's ideas into the area of public debate. In 1926 the War Office sanctioned the formation of a unit that would put these theories to the test. The Experimental Mechanized Force came into being on 1 May 1927 and can be regarded as the grandfather of all armoured divisions. Commanded by Colonel R. J. Collins, it consisted of a

Below: A Vickers light tank of 3rd Hussars, bogged down and blown apart by Italian artillery on the salt flats at Buq Buq, 12 December 1940. (IWM)

reconnaissance group equipped with tankettes and armoured cars, a battalion of 48 Vickers medium tanks, a motorized machine-gun battalion, a mechanized artillery regiment, which included one battery of fully tracked self-propelled guns, and a motorized engineer field company. During the subsequent exercise its speed and flexibility virtually paralysed its conventional 'enemy' and its effect upon foreign military observers was electric; the United States and Soviet Russia quickly established similar formations and the Germans, who were currently denied tanks under the terms of the Treaty of Versailles, were deeply impressed. The Experimental Mechanized Force also took part in the 1928 manoeuvres but was then disbanded. The year 1931 saw the formation of 1 Tank Brigade consisting of three battalions and commanded by Brigadier Charles Broad. This took the work of the Experimental Mechanized Force a stage further in that its

units were controlled on the move by voice radio.

Meanwhile, in 1929 work had begun on the mechanization of the cavalry. In 1934 its Inspector-General stated frankly that he could see no future for horsed cavalry and requested that most of his regiments be converted to armour. By 1939 only four regular cavalry regiments retained their horses. As the war clouds began to gather the RTC had been expanded and Territorial battalions were formed while a number of Yeomanry armoured car companies were enlarged to regimental strength. In 1939 these various elements were amalgamated to form the Royal Armoured Corps, although their individual identities were preserved, the former RTC battalions becoming Royal Tank Regiments.

By the mid-1930s the War Office had formulated a policy for the employment of tanks and in 1938 the first of two mobile divisions was formed. The following year

Below: An A.9 cruiser tank of 1 RTR photographed in Cairo shortly before the war spread to North Africa. The markings on the front of the vehicle show the unit's tactical number, the 12-ton bridge classification and the white circle on red square which was the 7th Armoured Division's first insignia. (RAC Tank Museum)

these were designated armoured divisions, the 1st being stationed in the United Kingdom and the 7th in Egypt. During this period their organization consisted of a light armoured brigade of three regiments equipped with cruiser and light tanks; a heavy armoured brigade of three regiments equipped with cruiser tanks; and a support group containing a motorized rifle battalion, a motorized artillery regiment and an engineer company. In 1940 the distinction between the two armoured brigades was abandoned and the support group received a second rifle battalion and a mixed anti-tank/anti-aircraft regiment; somewhat later in the year an armoured car regiment was added to the divisional establishment. Support for infantry operations was to be the responsibility of specialist army tank brigades, each consisting of three regiments equipped with infantry tanks. The light tank, which had performed well in the outposts of

Empire, was also to be used for reconnaissance by the infantry's divisional cavalry regiments.

It was, unfortunately, one thing to formulate policy and draft formation establishments, but quite another to give these substance, for by 1936 most of the United Kingdom's tank stock was obsolete. New designs were on their way, but even in those comparatively unsophisticated days the period between the drawing-board and quantity production phases was considerable. On the outbreak of war the British Army possessed approximately 1,150 tanks, of which the majority were lights. There were also some A-9 and A-13 cruiser tanks with 14mm frontal armour, a few slower A-10 cruisers with 30mm armour, and a number of Infantry Tanks Mks I and II with, respectively, 60mm and 78mm armour. With the exception of the Infantry Tank Mk I, which mounted a single machine-gun, these were armed

Below: The A.13 cruiser tank employed the Christie suspension. Additional protection for the turret walls was obtained by fitting angled plating which would blunt the impact of the enemy's shot before it reached the main armour. This feature was inherited by the A.15 cruiser tank, better known as the Crusader. (RAC Tank Museum)

with the 2pdr gun and one or more machine-guns. The situation would improve steadily but even so on 10 May 1940, the date on which the German offensive in the west began, the only British armoured units serving in France were one armoured car regiment, seven divisional cavalry regiments with light tanks, and the incomplete 1 Army Tank Brigade with two regiments. The 1st Armoured Division, well below strength, was still in the United Kingdom, but in Egypt the 7th Armoured Division, trained to the peak of efficiency the previous year by Major-General P. C. S. Hobart, was in a much healthier state.

FRANCE

At the end of the Great War the French had more tanks than anyone else and, notwithstanding developments elsewhere, were regarded as the experts on armoured warfare for the next twenty years. In 1920 responsibility for tanks was transferred from the artillery to the infantry where, in the main, it rested until the disasters of 1940. There were, of course, progressive thinkers in the French Army, notably General J. E. Estienne, the father of French armour; Colonel Romain and, later, Colonel Charles de Gaulle, who advocated the formation of armoured divisions, but they were swimming against a tide of opinion led by no less a person than Marshal Philippe Pétain, the successful defender of that symbol of French honour and determination, Verdun.

The French cavalry, however, were also interested in tanks. In 1917 each cavalry division had been assigned a unit of eighteen armoured cars, this figure being doubled in 1923. Mechanization of the cavalry continued slowly but steadily until in 1930 one of the division's three mounted brigades was replaced by a lorried infantry regiment the members of which were known as *Dragons Portés*, and part of the divisional artillery was motorized. In 1932 the armoured element of the division became a regiment with a total of eighty AFVs, including a number of tanks. By 1934 a fully mechanized cavalry division existed and this was designated the *1ère Division*

Below: The Renault AMC (Type ACG1) served with French cavalry formations. It was armed with a semi-automatic 25mm cannon and had a maximum speed of 25mph. (RAC Tank Museum)

Above: Captured French tanks, like this Renault R35, were unsuitable for employment within the German panzer divisions and were used by occupation troops in various parts of Europe. (RAC Tank Museum)

Légère Mécanique (DLM). In May 1940 three DLMs were operational and a fourth was in process of forming. Their organization consisted of a reconnaissance regiment with two armoured car and two motor-cycle squadrons; a tank brigade of two regiments, equipped with Somuas and H-35s; a motor rifle brigade of three battalions, each with an organic light tank company of twenty AMRs, a motor-cycle company, two lorried infantry companies and a heavy weapons company; a motorized artillery regiment and an engineer battalion. The functions of the DLMs were those traditionally associated with the cavalry: the provision of a screen behind which the main body of the army could deploy, strategic reconnaissance and exploitation after a victory.

In the infantry, too, thoughts were turning towards the concentrated use of tanks to reinforce assaults on the more important axes of advance. Such groupings, referred to as *chars de manoeuvre d'ensemble*, would employ only the most powerful infantry tanks and be allocated to corps and divisional commanders as the situation warranted. In September 1939 this concept led to the formation of the *1ère Division Cuirassée* (DCR), which consisted of two armoured demi-brigades (each with one battalion of 34 Char B heavy tanks and one battalion of 45 H-35s), one battalion of motorized riflemen and two 12-gun groups of motorized artillery. By May 1940 three DCRs had been formed and a fourth, commanded by de Gaulle, was assembling. Unfortunately, the component elements of these formations were unused to working together and the training of the DCRs was incomplete when the German offensive began. Equally unfortunate was the fact that no higher formation, i.e., corps headquarters were formed to co-ordinate the operations of either the DCRs or DLMs.

The essential flaw afflicting the two major types of armoured formation possessed by the French Army was that each performed a different function, the

Left: The Char B, protected by 60mm armour and armed with a 47mm gun in the turret and a 75mm howitzer in the bow, formed the backbone of the *Divisions Cuirassées*. The Germans found it a formidable opponent, but its vulnerable tracks and radiator louvres, heavy fuel consumption and one-man turret proved to be fatal flaws. (RAC Tank Museum)

Left: The Somua S35, armed with a 47mm gun, served with the French Army's *Divisions Légères Mécaniques*. (RAC Tank Museum)

Right: Up-gunned Hotchkiss H39 used against the Allies in western Europe, 1944. Note the undischarged Panzerfaust wedged against the spade on the track guard. (RAC Tank Museum)

DCRs being designed specifically to achieve a breakthrough and the DLMs for a more open style of mobile warfare. In contrast, the German panzer divisions performed both roles as a matter of course.

When fighting began in earnest the French Army possessed approximately 3,000 tanks, of which more than two-thirds were of comparatively modern design. The most impressive tank in French service was the Char B, armed with a limited-traverse 75mm howitzer in the bow plate, a 47mm gun in the turret and two machine-guns. The Char B had a maximum speed of 17mph and was protected by 60mm armour, but its fuel consumption was heavy and its tracks were vulnerable, as were the radiator louvres housed in the left wall of the hull. About 320 of these vehicles, which the out-gunned and under-protected Germans were to name *Kolosse*, were available on 10 May 1940. The DLMs' Somua S-35, with its 55mm armour, turret-mounted 47mm main armament and 25mph maximum speed, was in many respects an even better design. Altogether, the French had 500 tanks serving with the

DCRs and 800 with the DLMs and mounted cavalry divisions, the remainder of their less impressive tank fleet being allocated to infantry support battalions deployed along the front.

The provision of good guns and stout armour for their better tank designs was, however, counter-balanced by the French Army's decision to adopt the one-man turret as standard. This meant that the vehicle commander was simultaneously responsible for loading, laying and firing the turret weapons, directing his driver, navigating, choosing good tactical ground and perhaps controlling the actions of subordinate tanks. Inevitably, such tasks would be performed under pressure and their combined effect was to demand more mental agility than most men possessed, the result being that the efficiency of overworked commanders tended to decline rapidly once action was joined. Significantly, both the British and the Germans preferred three-man turret crews for their medium tanks, and most other nations set the minimum requirement at two.

SOVIET UNION

For the first years of its life the only tanks that the Soviet Army could field were elderly British and French models captured from the White armies during the Civil War; incredible as it may seem, in 1928 the Soviet tank strength amounted to a mere 92 machines, all of them obsolete. Then came a series of Five Year Plans which rationalized tank manufacture to such an extent that by 1935 there were in excess of 10,000 tanks in service, and by 1941, the year Hitler invaded the USSR, the figure had risen to 24,000. During this period a number of trends appeared that were to remain constant features of Russian tank design, including the adoption of the V-12 aluminium alloy diesel engine, the provision of wide tracks for driving in the worst conditions that deep snow and the mud of the spring thaw could produce, and the mounting of larger calibre guns than could generally be found on the tanks of other armies. A wide variety of tank types was produced, including the multi-turreted T-100 and T-35 heavy tanks intended for the breakthrough role, one such machine

provoking a rare flash of humour from Stalin, who commented that it resembled a department store; the T-26 and somewhat larger T-28 for direct infantry support; the fast BT Series, based on the Christie suspension, for deep penetration operations; and the amphibious T-37, T-38 and T-40 tankette/light tank series for reconnaissance. The performance of many of these vehicles fell far short of their designers' intentions, but the technical lessons learned resulted in the development of the superb T-34 medium tank and the heavily armoured KV (*Klimenti Voroshilov*) heavy tank series, both of which entered service in 1940.

Notwithstanding the remarkable progress made by Russian tank designers, notably Mikhail Koshkin and Iosef Kotin, the Soviet armoured corps entered the Second World War lacking a viable doctrine. In part, the reasons for this stemmed from internal political tensions, but the failure of inexperienced commanders to interpret events correctly was also a major contributory factor. Nevertheless, the proportion of progressive thinkers was as high in the Soviet Army as in any other. In 1927 an artillery officer,

Below: Abandoned T-35 heavy tank being examined by members of the Wehrmacht. The vehicle was fitted with no less than five turrets, one mounting a short 76.2mm howitzer, two with 45mm guns and two with 7.62mm machine-guns. Steering failures were common because of the great length of track in contact with the ground. This example is fitted with a frame antenna around its turret and is evidently a command vehicle. (IWM)

Right: Soviet T-40 amphibious light tank. Few survived the débâcles of 1941. (IWM)

Right: Although the photograph suggests that the function of the BT series was reconnaissance, it had been designed specifically for deep penetration operations. (IWM)

V. K. Triandafillov, published a book entitled *The Character of the Operations of Modern Armies* in which he quoted Fuller's ideas and stressed the need for surprise at every level, the generation of intense violence on a limited frontage to obtain a rapid breakthrough, followed by a high-speed advance to the strategic objective, emphasizing that mechanized formations must not allow themselves to become bogged down in the battles of their non-mechanized comrades. Triandafillov died shortly afterwards but his theories were welcomed by M. N. Tuckhachevsky, soon to become a Marshal of the Soviet Union. Both officers were products of the Tsar's army which, like the German Army, did not think simply in terms of strategy, i.e., the planning of a campaign, and tactics, its execution at local level by the troops on the ground, but interposed an intermediate or operative level devoted to the conduct of operations at corps level, although this could extend as high as army. Not surprisingly, therefore, Tuckhachevsky chose to form mechanized corps rather than divisions, and the first of these appeared in 1932. They consisted of two or three mechanized brigades, each of three tank battalions and an infantry battalion with light automatic weapons, a motorized infantry brigade and a motorized artillery regiment.

Tuckhachevsky's mechanized corps have been criticized for having too high a ratio of tanks to mechanized infantry, although most contemporary armies made the same mistake. More important was the lack of an adequate command and communications apparatus because this meant that once a formation was committed to action its commander was unable to control it in circumstances that might be radically different from those existing when the operation was planned. This stemmed partly from a serious shortage of tank radio sets, partly from the low level of secondary technical education which was unable to produce the operators to man them, and partly because of a rigid command structure imposed by a political system which preferred centralized planning to personal initiative.

Given time, Tuckhachevsky could probably have eliminated most of these defects, but Stalin saw him as a dangerous rival. In June 1937 Tuckhachevsky and his principal supporters were arrested, court-marshalled and shot. The Soviet officer corps was then ruthlessly purged from top to bottom, thousands being executed or sent to labour camps on the merest suspicion of disloyalty. Those who survived the Great Purge were too cowed to do more than passively await orders from above and then obey them to the letter. This was to have a disastrous effect on the conduct of Soviet armoured operations during the early years of the war. Furthermore, the mechanized corps were disbanded and their tank units re-assigned to infantry support, largely on the recommendation of General D. G. Pavlov, the commander of the Russian tank force which had been sent to assist the Republican government during

the Spanish Civil War. In fact, Pavlov's tanks had broken through into the enemy's hinterland on several occasions but had always been forced to withdraw; what he had failed to grasp was that had they been accompanied by motorized infantry and artillery the captured ground could have been consolidated and a favourable situation further exploited. As it was, he took the view that deep penetration operations, and indeed the use of armour at the operative level, had been discredited, and Stalin was only too pleased to accept his advice.

In September 1939 the Soviet Army invaded eastern Poland while hostilities were still in progress between that country and Germany. The clumsy handling of the demoralized Russian armour, followed by its lack-lustre performance during the 1939–40 Winter War against Finland, gave the Germans a false impression of Soviet potential and was a factor taken into account when planning their invasion of the USSR in 1941.

In Manchuria, however, General Georgi Zhukov had chosen to fight a battle in the Tuckhachevsky mould and in August 1939 had inflicted a sharp defeat on the

Below: The BT series of Soviet cruiser tanks employed the Christie suspension. Unusual features included a steering wheel and the ability to run on tracks or wheels alone. (IWM)

Left: The T-26 light tank was based on a Vickers design and was employed in support of infantry operations. (IWM)

Left: In 1941 the German Army did not possess a tank gun capable of defeating the thick armour of the KV1 heavy tank. Initially, the KV1 made an even greater impression on its opponents than the T-34/76, until the latter's secrets were revealed.

Japanese at the River Khalkhin. Faced with the evidence of this and the example set by the German panzer corps in Poland and the west, Stalin and Pavlov had no alternative but to re-form the recently disbanded mechanized corps. The new corps contained two tank divisions, each consisting of two tank regiments with a total of 400 BTs, T-34s and KVs, a motorized infantry regiment and a motorized artillery regiment; and one motorized infantry division containing two motorized infantry

regiments, one tank regiment and one motorized artillery regiment. It was planned to form twenty such corps by the autumn of 1941, but the German invasion in June of that year caught the Soviet armour in the throes of reorganization. Those corps that were formed would have been regarded as unwieldy even had adequate communications existed, and they had had little opportunity for training. They were, moreover, commanded by officers who were more frightened of Stalin and his

Right: The T-34/76 provided a balanced combination of firepower protection and mobility. The confidence of German armoured units was severely jolted by the discovery that the Soviet Army was capable of producing so advanced a concept in tank design. (IWM)

Party *apparatchiks* than they were of the enemy, and a high proportion of their tanks were off the road with mechnical problems.

Thus, despite possessing more tanks than the rest of the world's armies put together, the Soviet armoured corps was in very poor shape for the ordeal which lay ahead. The best that could be said was that the newer 76.2mm tank guns, coupled with the 90/110mm armour of the KV and the 45mm armour of the T-34, the latter laid back to provide the equivalent of 90mm protection, would provide the Wehrmacht with a most unpleasant surprise and influence tank design for many years to come.

UNITED STATES

In 1919 the US Army's Tank Corps was disbanded as a separate arm of service and the following year the National Defense Act confirmed that tank development, training and tactics were to be the sole responsibility of the Chief of Infantry, the tank's primary mission being defined as 'to facilitate the uninterrupted advance of the rifleman in the attack'. Some voices were raised in protest, including those of Major

George S. Patton, Jr, a cavalry officer who had seen active service with tanks on the Western Front, and Major David D. Eisenhower, but the official reaction was that these individuals would either remain silent on the subject or suffer irreparable damage to their careers.

In 1927, however, the Secretary of War, Dwight F. Davis, visited the United Kingdom and witnessed the exercises carried out by the Experimental Mechanized Force. On his return he ordered the Chief of Staff to organize a similar force and in 1928 this assembled at Fort Meade, Maryland, consisting of one heavy and one light tank battalion, a motorized infantry battalion, an artillery battalion armed with 75mm guns carried *portée* on trucks, an engineer company and a signals company. Thanks largely to the use of obsolete equipment the experiment fell short of being an unqualified success and after three months the force was disbanded.

Having shed its heavy tank element and added another infantry battalion to its establishment, the Mechanized Force assembled again at Fort Eustis, Virginia, in 1930. This time it fulfilled its mission, which was to demonstrate the benefits of

mechanization to the rest of the Army. General Douglas MacArthur, who became Chief of Staff in 1931, was himself an advocate of mechanization and did not disband the Mechanized Force until the following year, when the major part of it moved to Fort Knox, Kentucky, to form the nucleus of a mechanized cavalry regiment.

It was, in fact, in the cavalry that the more progressive views on armoured warfare were to be found. As a result of the urgings of the then Colonel Adna Chaffee and like-minded officers, its armoured cars were eventually supplemented with light tanks, which it called combat cars to avoid falling foul of the National Defense Act, and with these demonstrated the possibilities of wide-ranging operations in armour. The 7th Cavalry Brigade (Mechanized), the US Army's first armoured formation, was formed in 1932 but remained incomplete until 1939, when its establishment consisted of two mechanized cavalry regiments with a total of 112 light tanks and a motorized artillery regiment with 75mm howitzers, a lorried infantry regiment being attached for the 1940 spring manoeuvres in Louisiana.

The smashing victories won by the German armour in Poland and western Europe convinced the War Department that the hitherto separate interests of the infantry and the cavalry should be combined and on 10 July 1940 the Armored Force was created with Brigadier-General Chaffee as its first Chief. A week later I Armored Corps was formed from the 1st and 2nd Armored Divisions, which had been activated on 15 July, the former having absorbed the 7th Cavalry Brigade (Mechanized). In its original form the American armoured division contained an armoured brigade consisting of two light tank regiments each of three battalions and one two-battalion medium tank regiment, plus a two-battalion artillery regiment equipped with self-propelled 105mm howitzers; a two-battalion motorized infantry battalion; an additional artillery battalion; an armoured reconnaissance battalion; an engineer battalion and the usual divisional service units. This organization was revised in March 1942, the most important change being the replacement of the armoured brigade headquarters with two Combat Commands, 'A' and 'B', each of which could be allocated units by the divisional commander for particular tasks, thereby permitting greater flexibility than had hitherto been possible. The 1942 revision also went some way to reducing the tank-heavy aspect of the division, which now contained two armoured regiments each with one light and two medium tank battalions; an armored infantry regiment of three battalions; three artillery battalions equipped with 105mm self-propelled howitzers; an armoured reconnaissance battalion; an engineer battalion and divisional services.

During the inter-war years the army had been so starved of funds that it had only been able to produce one or two experimental prototype tanks per year, accompanied by relatively short production runs of the few designs that had been standardized. In July 1940, therefore, the infant Armored Force found itself in possession of some 500 machines, the majority of which were hopelessly obsolete. On the other hand, the recently standardized M-3 Light Tank (Stuart) was a good design for its weight and the M-2 Medium, intended for infantry support, was developed into the M-3 Medium (Lee), armed with a sponson-mounted 75mm gun, at very short notice, while the design of a main battle tank with a turret-mounted 75mm gun, the M-4 (Sherman), was well in hand. To this, of course, must be added the United States' enormous industrial capacity which would guarantee production well beyond American requirements.

Right: Medium Tank M3 Lee of the US 1st Armored Division shortly after arriving in North Africa. (USAMHI)

Left: The Light Tank M5 incorporated a number of improvements on the basic M3 design, but was still known as the Stuart. The photograph, taken near Maknassy, Tunisia, shows an M5 of Company 'A', 899th Tank Destroyer Battalion. (US Army Military History Institute)

Right: The Medium Tank M4 Sherman became the US Army's standard battle tank and first saw action with the British Eighth Army during the Second Battle of Alamein. The squadron shown here is equipped with the M4A1 version. (RAC Tank Museum)

GERMANY

Forbidden tanks under the terms of the Treaty of Versailles, the German Army had perforce to obtain its experience by clandestine means, which it did by concluding a mutually beneficial secret agreement with the USSR under which an AFV testing station was established deep inside Russia. Concurrently, experimental work was carried out discreetly in Sweden, resulting in the accumulation of much useful technical data.

Discussion of armoured warfare within the 100,000-strong professional Reichsheer polarized into conservative and progressive schools of thought, just as it did in other armies, but with the difference that it took place in the context of the traditional German strategic design known as *Vernichtungsgedanke*, the Annihilation Concept. This involved the initiation of a mobile battle with the object of falling on one or both of the enemy's flanks with a view to encircling and destroying his army piecemeal, and it was deeply embedded in the thought processes of the generation of former Imperial officers who had learned their profession in the shadow of the great von Moltke and were now controlling Germany's armed forces. The question was, when Germany acquired tanks in due course, were they to be used in support of the older arms to fulfil the concept, or were they capable of fulfilling it on their own?

One officer who had no doubts that the latter was the case was the then Captain Heinz Guderian, a former light infantryman and communications specialist who, in 1922, was serving in the Transport Troops Inspectorate. Here he began to read avidly whatever books he could obtain on the subject of armoured warfare and later commented that: 'It was principally the books and articles of the Englishmen, Fuller, Liddell Hart and Martel, that excited my interest and gave me food for thought. I learned from them the concentration of armour, as employed in the Battle of Cambrai. Further, it was Liddell Hart who emphasized the use of armoured forces for long-range strokes, operations against the opposing army's communications, and also proposed a type of armoured division combining panzer and panzer-infantry units. Deeply impressed by these ideas. I tried to develop them in a sense practicable for our own army.'

In fact, it took very little imagination to see that the ideas of Fuller and Liddell Hart

Below: Pz Kpfw Is take part in a pre-war exercise. Although it was produced as a training vehicle, the Pz Kpfw I saw extensive active service during the German Army's campaigns 1939–41. (RAC Tank Museum)

dovetailed with *Vernichtungsgedanke*, the only major difference being that the emphasis was shifted from the enemy's flank to deep within his rear. Guderian began writing articles of his own and soon became well known for his views, which he continued to press on senior officers as he rose slowly up the promotion ladder. Some supported him, some were sympathetic but frankly doubted whether the tanks of the period were capable of delivering what he promised, and a few were bluntly antagonistic. He remained in the forefront of the debate, and history has justly awarded him the credit for his perseverence, but it must be remembered that his widely read memoirs, *Panzer Leader*, provide a very personal view of the period, and that they are far from free of personal prejudice.

There were a number of senior officers who were equally interested in the new ideas and were actually able to influence events. In 1926, for example, Major-General Alfred von Vollard-Bockelberg took over the Transport Troops Inspectorate and the following year began training mechanical transport officers in the theory of armoured warfare, based on the British Army pamphlet *Provisional Instructions for Armoured Vehicles 1927*, holding exercises with mock-up cardboard tanks mounted on automobile chassis. In 1929 he moved to the Ordnance Department, where he remained until the end of 1933, during which period he accelerated the process of mechanization within the army, formed the first motor-cycle and mechanized reconnaissance units and set in motion the design phase of what were to

Right: Driver's controls and instrument panel, Pz Kpfw I Model A. The steering levers also served as a parking brake. (RAC Tank Museum)

become Germany's first mass-produced tanks, the Pz Kpfw I and II.

During the early 1930s the idea of armoured formations found favour with the War Minister, General von Blomberg, the Chief of the Reichswehr Ministerial Office, Colonel-General Walter von Reichenau, with whom Guderian got on extremely well, and the Army's Commander-in-Chief from 1 February 1934, Colonel-General Freiherr von Fritsch. Of General Ludwig Beck, the Chief of General Staff 1935–38, Guderian's scathing comments are as unfair as they are vindictive, for while Beck may have made clear his obvious dislike of Guderian, he was far from hostile to new ideas and indeed it was during his period of office that the first panzer divisions were formed and the foundation of the Sturmartillerie laid.

The Nazi Party was voted into power in January 1933. On 16 March 1935 Hitler renounced the restrictive clauses of the Treaty of Versailles and declared that Germany would re-arm as she thought fit.

On 15 October of that year the first three panzer divisions began assembling, the second commanded by Guderian. Their organization included a panzer brigade consisting of two regiments each of two battalions, each battalion containing one heavy and three light/medium companies, giving a total theoretical tank strength of 562 vehicles, which never approached reality; a motorized infantry brigade consisting of one two-battalion lorried infantry regiment and a motor-cycle battalion; a motorized artillery regiment; an armoured reconnaissance battalion which included two armoured car squadrons, a motor-cycle machine-gun squadron and a heavy weapons squadron; plus anti-tank, engineer and signals battalions, joined later by an anti-aircraft battalion, and divisional service units. The 4th and 5th Panzer Divisions were formed in 1938, followed by the 10th in April 1940.

The older arms, too, demanded their share of armour, and this absorbed an unwelcome proportion of the already

Below: Pz Kpfw I of the independent panzer battalion (Pz Abt zbV 40) which took part in the 1940 campaign in Norway. (US National Archives)

Right: Pz Kpfw II of 3rd Panzer Division batters its way through a makeshift barricade, France 1940. (US National Archives)

Below: Mine-damaged Pz Kpfw I abandoned in the Western Desert. Comparatively few of these vehicles were sent to North Africa. (RAC Tank Museum)

Above: Pz Kpfw II of 8th Panzer Division halted at the roadside during Operation 'Barbarossa'. (US National Archives)

unsatisfactory tank production figures which would otherwise have benefited the panzer divisions. Two independent panzer brigades and an independent panzer regiment were formed specifically to support infantry operations. The cavalry, most of which had been mechanized but which still performed its traditional functions, also required tanks for its four light divisions, which were formed in 1938 and were similar to the French DLMs. The establishment of these divisions included one panzer battalion, four motor-rifle battalions and reconnaissance, artillery and engineer elements.

Such diversions, however, were comparatively short-lived. The Sturmartil-lerie, equipped with assault guns based on the chassis of the Pz Kpfw III, was established as a separate branch of service which would specialize in direct infantry support, and although its first batteries were not available for active service until the spring of 1940, in the interim the infantry support tank units were absorbed into panzer divisions. After the 1939 campaign in Poland the establishment of the light

divisions were expanded and they became the 6th, 7th, 8th and 9th Panzer Divisions.

As has been mentioned already, the German Army placed great importance on the conduct of operations at the operative level, and it was therefore quite natural that the panzer divisions should be grouped together in panzer corps, and that panzer corps should be formed into panzer groups which would later be redesignated panzer armies. The effect of this was to give German field commanders a weapon of concentrated power which other armies could not hope to match. Conversely, the German Army itself became a two-tier structure in which the armoured and motorized formations possessed an infinitely superior mobility to the great marching mass which still relied on the horse as the prime mover for its artillery and transport wagons.

Even before Hitler repudiated the Treaty of Versailles, Germany had produced a few prototype tanks under the thin cover story that they were tractors or construction plant. In 1935, however, she was forced to equip the Panzerwaffe from scratch and the

Above: Pz Kpfw III Model A in Poland, 1939. Because of the soft going in the frontier areas many German tanks carried a small fascine. (Bundesarchiv)

Ordnance Department indicated a requirement for four different types of vehicle, production of which began at once. The Pz Kpfw I, armed with twin machine-guns, was an intentionally simple little machine intended for basic crew training. The Pz Kpfw II, armed with a 20mm cannon and a coaxial machine-gun, was a slightly larger light tank which was conceived as a reconnaissance vehicle but in the event was required to perform a much wider role. The Pz Kpfw III, armed with a 37mm gun and secondary machine-guns, was intended as the main battle tank which would equip three of the panzer battalion's four companies. Senior tank officers, aware that the British were fitting the 40mm 2pdr gun to their new Cruiser tanks and that the Russian BTs and T-26s already mounted a 45mm gun, had initially requested that the vehicle be armed with a 50mm gun, but the Ordnance Department, supported by the Artillery Inspectorate, pointed out that the infantry were already in possession of the 37mm anti-tank gun, and the obvious benefits of standardization. The discussion resulted in a compromise in which the

37mm was fitted while the turret ring was made wide enough to accommodate the 50mm if the need arose. The fourth tank, the Pz Kpfw IV, which was to equip the panzer battalion's fourth or heavy company, was armed with a short 75mm howitzer, the idea being that the direct fire of this weapon with high-explosive ammunition would eliminate the enemy's anti-tank guns from a range beyond the latter's ability to make effective reply.

The Pz Kpfw III and IV were essentially sound designs, but their development was hampered by suspension problems and they were being produced in such small numbers that it is unlikely that Hitler could have gone to war in 1939 had not he acquired the Czech tank fleet and manufacturing capacity. Two Czech medium tank designs, both armed with a 37mm gun which enabled them to be substituted for the Pz Kpfw III, were available in quantity and were taken into German service as the Pz Kpfw 35(t) and Pz Kpfw 38(t). Even so, light tanks continued to form the bulk of German tank strength until approximately the end of 1941.

Above: Pz Kpfw II (left) and Pz Kpfw 38(t) command tank of regimental headquarters 25th Panzer Regiment (7th Panzer Division), France 1940.

Left: Pz Kpfw 35(t) of 6th Panzer Division advance into Russia 1941. (US National Archives)

Above: Pz Kpfw IV stalled in a ford. The photograph was probably taken in Germany during the winter of 1939/40 because the vehicle is marked with the black national cross introduced after the Polish campaign, and the crew are still wearing their padded berets, soon to be replaced by the forage cap. The Pz Kpfw IV, armed with a 75mm L/24 howitzer, served in the close support role during the first half of the war. (RAC Tank Museum)

Guderian's star continued to rise rapidly and on 20 November 1938 he was promoted General der Panzertruppen and appointed Chief of Mobile Troops. As a former signals specialist he was well aware of the connection between operational flexibility and good communications and it was at his insistence that every tank was fitted for radio, and armoured command vehicles were developed for the various command levels. The closest possible links were also established with the Luftwaffe's ground-attack wings which would provide the panzer divisions with on-call air support.

Much emphasis was laid on the fact that the panzer division was a balanced formation designed for offensive use and that much of its success would depend upon its ability to generate violence during the break-through phase. Similarly, it was stressed that once divisions were through the enemy's defended zone, which would be penetrated on a comparatively narrow divisional frontage of not more than 5,000 yards, they would accelerate towards their strategic objective, regardless of what was taking place elsewhere. Anti-tank guns

were to be used aggressively in a 'sword-and-shield' technique which involved the German tanks retiring through anti-tank gun screens if they were counter-attacked by enemy armour, then counter-attacking in turn once the enemy's strength had been written down.

Some practical knowledge of modern war was obtained by the Condor Legion, the German contingent dispatched by Hitler to support Franco's Nationalists during the Spanish Civil War. The German experience was similar to the Russian but it was appreciated that this was not a contest between first-class armies, and erroneous conclusions were avoided. The Pz Kpfw I proved inadequate as a combat vehicle and, whenever possible, its numbers were supplemented by captured Russian BTs and T-26s. Again, the bloodless occupations of Austria and Czechoslovakia provided the Panzerwaffe with lessons which were put to good use in increasing its operational efficiency.

In September 1939 the Panzerwaffe went to war with approximately 3,200 tanks, but of these 1,445 were Pz Kpfw Is and 1,223 Pz

Kpfw IIs; only 98 Pz Kpfw IIIs and 211 Pz Kpfw IVs were available, the balance being made up by Czech vehicles. Despite this, it alone of the world's armoured corps had a viable operational doctrine and the means to apply it, and, over the next two years, this was to win easy victories in Poland, France, the Balkans and the Soviet Union, often in the face of apparently insuperable odds. The speed with which these victories were won was to add a new word to the language of warfare – *Blitzkrieg*.

ITALY

The Italian Army formed its Corpo Carristi (Armoured Corps) in 1926. This was equipped for the first few years of its life with the Fiat 3000, a locally produced version of the French Renault FT, of which 180 were built. During the early 1930s, however, Carden Loyd tankettes were adopted as a quick and easy means of boosting Italy's tank strength. Armed with one or two machine-guns, the tankette series was originally designated by the letters CV (*Carro Veloce* – Fast Tank), amended to L (*Leggiero* – Light) in 1938. They were allocated to cavalry groups and infantry support battalions despite the fact that their 13mm armour rendered them quite unsuitable for the latter role.

In 1936 a mechanized brigade was formed, including a light tank battalion, a motorized Bersaglieri regiment, a motorized artillery battery and an engineer section. The following year this establishment was expanded to include a tank regiment with up to four light battalions, a motorized Bersaglieri regiment, two anti-tank companies, an anti-aircraft battery and an engineer company, the formation being redesignated 1st Armoured Brigade. The 2nd Armoured Brigade was formed shortly after and in February 1939 this became the 132nd Armoured Division 'Ariete'. In April the 131st Armoured Division 'Centauro' was formed from the 1st Armoured Brigade, followed by the 133rd Armoured Division 'Littorio', which began assembling later that year. In theory the divisional establishment consisted of one four-battalion tank regiment, a Bersaglieri

regiment with one motor-cycle and one lorried infantry battalion, a motorized artillery regiment, an anti-aircraft troop and an engineer company. In practice, the tank regiment had only one light and one medium tank battalion, each of two companies. Furthermore, the recently developed M-11/39 three-man medium tank was a bad design in which the 37mm main armament was housed in a sponson remote from the commander's control, and was in short supply. It can thus be seen that while the three armoured divisions had been formed to execute the Italian version of the *Blitzkrieg* technique, the *guerra di rapido corso*, they were fundamentally weak organizations.

Italian armour saw action in Ethiopia in 1934–5, where an imaginative development was the supply of advance columns by parachute drop, and during the Spanish Civil War, in which its tankettes were hopelessly outclassed by their Russian opponents. Some armoured units also took part in the unopposed occupation of Albania in April 1939.

Italy did not declare war on the United Kingdom and France until 10 June 1940. During the early fighting in southern France, Libya and East Africa the Italian armour consisted of the infantry divisions' organic tankette battalions and similarly equipped cavalry units. One M-11/39 battalion was sent to East Africa and two

Above: Gutted M13/40 medium tank lies beside a burned-out Churchill of Kingforce on the Alamein battlefield. (IWM)

more to Libya, followed by several more medium tank battalions armed with the new M-13/40, which was already verging on obsolescence but at least mounted a 47mm gun housed in a conventional turret. These were formed into an armoured brigade but this was committed piecemeal and was destroyed at Beda Fomm in February 1941.

JAPAN

The Japanese Army, like the Italian, never really recovered from the slow start it made in developing its armoured force. After the First World War a number of British and French designs were purchased for evaluation, but it was not until 1929 that a Japanese tank entered quantity production. This, the Type 89 medium tank, was armed with a short 57mm gun and two machine-guns and was intended for infantry support. Three infantry support regiments were formed in 1933, each with two companies of ten Type 89s. A fourth regiment, with three Type 89 companies,

was formed the following year as part of a spearhead formation known as the Independent Mixed Brigade, which also included motorized infantry and artillery regiments and an engineer company. The differing speeds of the various vehicles in this formation were not compatible and it was decided that the comparatively slow (15mph) Type 89 would be replaced by the much faster (28mph) Type 95 light tank, armed with a 37mm gun and two machine-guns, which had been under development since 1933. The Type 95 was to serve in every theatre of war where Japanese forces were engaged, but as far as the Independent Mixed Brigade was concerned it was regarded as a stop-gap pending the arrival of the new Type 97 medium tank, which was produced during the late 1930s in an attempt to match Western designs. The Type 97 was protected by 25mm armour, had a maximum speed of 25mph and was initially armed with the old 57mm gun, although this was later replaced by a 47mm high-velocity weapon. The remainder of the Japanese tank fleet consisted of tankettes of various sorts which were used to

Left: The Type 95 light tank, armed with a 37mm gun, was employed throughout the Pacific theatre of war. Like the Type 89, it was hopelessly outclassed by Allied armour. (RAC Tank Museum)

Left: The Type 97 medium tank, introduced in 1937, incorporated a number of interesting features and was armed with a short 57mm gun intended primarily for close support. Later models were fitted with a larger turret mounting a 47mm high-velocity gun, but by then the West had established an unassailable lead in tank technology. (RAC Tank Museum)

maintain supply lines between widely separated garrisons in China and Manchuria. In 1939 Japan possessed about 2,000 tanks, of which the great majority were in the light or tankette class.

The principal enemy of the Japanese armoured corps was complacency. Although a major conflict with China erupted in 1937, the Chinese were unable to offer serious opposition and the ability of the thin-skinned, under-gunned Japanese tanks to take their objectives without undue difficulty gave grounds for needless satisfaction. The sharp defeat inflicted by the Russians in Manchuria in 1939, coupled with the German victories in Europe, led to the formation of two armoured divisions on the Asian mainland, each based on a three-regiment armoured brigade equipped with Type 97s and Type 95s. In practice these were rarely up to strength, one or more tank regiments usually being detached for independent use.

FLEXIBILITY

It was already apparent during the inter-war years that even tank designs incorporating the best contemporary combinations of firepower, protection and mobility would fail to achieve their full potential on the battlefield unless they could be used with flexibility. Today, the exercise of this intangible but vital element is generally referred to as C3, meaning command, control and communications.

The tank attacks of the First World War were anything but flexible. Once the tanks had been given their objective and crossed their start-lines there was little that senior officers could do to control their movements; nor, for that matter, could the tanks report back on such subjects as bad going, obstacles, the nature of the resistance encountered and changed tactical situations. Often, battalion, company and section commanders exercised what control they could *on foot*, running between their vehicles under fire and telling the crews what was required. Significantly, the four Victoria Crosses won by officers of the Tank Corps were all awarded for dismounted actions that displayed supreme courage, total disregard for personal safety and outstanding leadership; Captain Clement Robertson, for example, chose to walk ahead of his tanks rather than have them lose their way over shell-torn going, but was shot dead just as they took their objective. Obviously, the loss of officers of this calibre was deplored as much as the means of applying tactical flexibility was desired. Various methods of solving the problem were tried, including carrier pigeons and semaphore arms, but none was satisfactory.

Hand flag signals made their appearance during the 1920s and in some armies, notably that of Soviet Russia, remained in use throughout the Second World War. These could create as many difficulties as they solved, however, as they not only identified the command vehicle and made it an immediate target, but also led to bunching by surbordinate units anxious for orders, thereby making the task of the enemy's gunners that much easier. In the Western Desert the British Army continued to fly recognition pennants and signal flags of different colours and shapes from its antennae. In theory these provided a means of communication during periods of enforced radio silence; in practice all flags viewed up-sun seemed to be black, pennants would be quickly ripped to tatters by a strong wind, and even turret-down vehicles could have their presence betrayed by bunting fluttering above the crest.

The radio provided the best means of achieving flexibility at all levels. Radios had, of course, existed during the First World War, and some had even been fitted to armoured vehicles, but they were bulky, had a very limited range and were unsuitable for use on the move. In the years that followed much technical progress was made to rectify these defects and in 1931 1 Brigade, Royal Tank Corps carried out a series of exercises on Salisbury Plain in which the movements of its 180 tanks were controlled by voice transmission. The benefits were so immediately obvious that by 1939 radios were standard issue throughout most of the world's major armoured corps, although Soviet Russia, Italy and Japan lagged far behind in their practical application.

The best tank radio sets combined three elements: an intercom or I/C unit which enabled the vehicle commander to talk to the driver and other members of his crew, a receiver, and a transmitter, the last two often being combined into a transceiver. Some armies maintained that only formation and unit commanders' tanks down to squadron/company level needed to be fitted with transceivers, and that receivers were good enough for the rest. In the event, however, battle damage and breakdowns quickly demonstrated that commanders often needed to change tanks and that effective control would be lost unless every vehicle were equipped with a transceiver. Unless special antennae were erected, and these were impractical for a formation on the move, the range of voice communication was still restricted to a few miles' radius, and at night the situation deteriorated as atmospheric interference intensified. Over longer distances and in poor conditions carrier wave transmissions using the Morse Code were employed, although the process was lengthy. Most armies preferred to locate their tank radios in the vehicle's hull, where it was operated by the otherwise under-employed hull gunner/co-driver. The British, on the other hand, located theirs in the rear of the turret, where it was the responsibility of the loader, thereby taking advantage of his proximity to the vehicle commander, who also had immediate access to the set if the need arose. For this reason the Royal Armoured Corps was unwilling to accept the American M3 Lee medium tank in its original form for service in the Western Desert, and insisted on a larger, re-designed turret, the composite vehicle being known as the Grant.

Transmissions were directed through radio nets, which existed at every appropriate level. The accompanying diagrams show in simplified form how commanders communicated with their own sub-units and supporting arms, as well as their rear link to the higher command net. Of particular importance are the

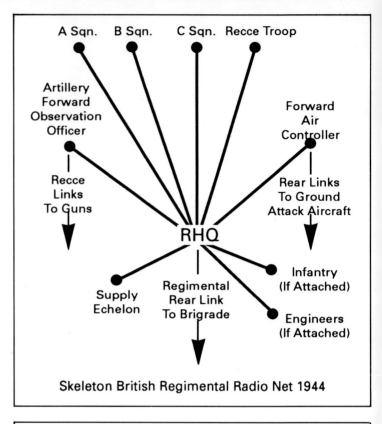

Skeleton British Regimental Radio Net 1944

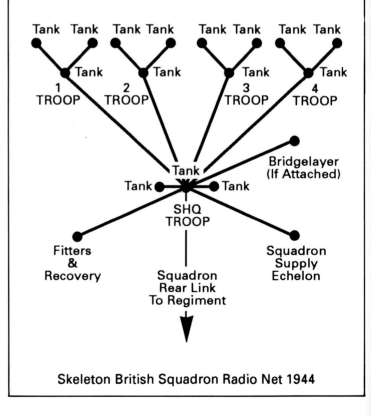

Skeleton British Squadron Radio Net 1944

commanders' link with their reconnaissance elements, which served as their
eyes and ears, and the rear links of the
artillery's forward observation officer
(FOO) and air force forward air controller
(FAC), who were to be found with the
leading elements and directed artillery fire
and tactical air support where it was
needed. Each station on the net had its own
call-sign, and standardized voice
procedures were used both to impose
discipline on crowded frequencies and to
make the job of the enemy's intercept
operators that much more difficult.

Despite these measures, plus the
transmission of vital information in code
and changes of frequency, the skill of
intercept operators was such that no net
could be regarded as secure for long. Bad or
sloppy procedure quickly enabled the
enemy to identify units in the line, their
approximate strength and even recognize
individuals by their faults. In this respect
senior officers were often the worst
offenders, since many had little previous
practical experience of radio and tended to
use it as a private telephone system. Veiled
speech concealed nothing and puzzled no
one; for example, Major-General Lloyd
Fredendall's mindless allusions to 'the
walking boys' and 'the big elephants' on
the US II Corps net in February 1943 could
hardly be references to anything other than
infantry and tanks. It was generally wise to
assume that the enemy had penetrated the
net and act accordingly, and with this in
mind British commanders with Indian
Army experience sometimes resorted to the
unconventional but effective means of
conversing with one another in Urdu. There
were occasions, too, when messages were
fatally corrupted during transmission. In
February 1945 Japanese senior officers
dismissed a report that a British column of
200 vehicles was advancing on the vital
communications centre of Meiktila in
Central Burma. The column actually
consisted of 17th Indian Division and 255
Indian Tank Brigade, and initially its
strength had been correctly assessed at
2,000 vehicles. Meiktila fell, with
catastrophic consequences for the
Japanese Burma Area Army.

Notwithstanding its shortcomings, and
these usually originated in its users, radio
conferred on commanders the ability to
deploy their units rapidly on the move, and
so accelerated the tempo at which
armoured operations were conducted.
Taking full advantage of this asset, the
commanders of the German panzer
divisions were able to detach all-arms
battle groups at little or no notice to execute
specific missions. Similarly, the Combat
Commands of the American armored
divisions could absorb and detach units as
the situation demanded. Prior to the Gazala
battle of May/June 1942 the British enjoyed
such flexibility that dispersion was
practised to an unacceptable degree. After
Montgomery had re-imposed orthodoxy on
the Eighth Army the emphasis lay on
maintaining the integrity of the armoured
division and the armoured brigade as
fighting formations. This in turn gave rise to
criticism that the Royal Armoured Corps
was somewhat less flexible than its German
or American counterparts, although given
the nature of the battles it was required to
fight in Italy, Normandy and north-west
Europe this was not immediately apparent,
nor did it affect their outcome. During the
final stages of the war in Burma, moreover,
British and Indian armoured formations
demonstrated an unsurpassed degree of
flexibility, forming mixed columns with
tanks, armoured cars, self-propelled
artillery and mechanized infantry which,
sometimes supplied by air drop, savaged
the enemy to destruction.

Those armoured corps that failed to apply
flexibility paid a terrible price for its
neglect. In 1940 the French armour
displayed less flexibility than did the
German, and although this was only one of
several factors that led to France's defeat it
was, none the less, extremely important, for
after the first shock of the *Blitzkrieg*
technique it never fully recovered its
balance. In February 1941 the Italian Tenth
Army, trapped by the British 7th Armoured
Division at Beda Fomm, attempted to fight
its way out of the ambush with a series of
tank attacks. These were unco-ordinated
and, since the issue of radios did not extend
below company commanders' vehicles,

lacked the flexibility enjoyed by their heavily out-numbered opponents, who were able to meet and defeat each attack in turn. After three days of fighting the Italians had lost most of their tanks and were forced to surrender.

In 1939 the Soviet armoured corps was the largest in the world, and also the least flexible. This stemmed in part from the effects of the Great Purge, which had left the officer corps cowed and unwilling to display initiative, partly from a political system which imposed centralized planning at every level of military life and, as previously mentioned, partly from a serious shortage of radio sets coupled with a low level of secondary technical education which was unable to produce sufficient operators to man them. In armoured units their issue did not extend below the level of battalion commander and this meant that operations had to be planned in detail and carefully rehearsed before they could be executed. Furthermore, the Party's dogma that only one correct solution existed for each problem was inherently flawed and totally

unsuited to the military context, where the nature of the problem itself was subject to constant change. Soviet attacks therefore possessed a rigidity comparable to that of the First World War and if they failed they were repeated until either the objective was taken or the troops involved were used up. In such circumstances the German armour exploited its own flexibility by mounting counter-attacks into the Soviet flanks and rear areas. Even if offensives mounted in this manner did succeed, the cost in personnel casualties and gutted tanks was so horrific that the most dedicated Leninist theoretician was compelled to change his views. Thousands of tank radio sets were supplied by the Western Allies but such was the scale of the conflict on the Eastern Front that these barely kept pace with wastage.

A partial answer was found by attaching senior staff officers to the various formation headquarters down the chain of command and permitting these to sanction local variations, provided they did not conflict with the overall plan. From the middle of 1943 onwards these measures resulted in a

Below: When ordering the Medium Tank M3 the British Tank Commission insisted on a larger turret capable of housing the tank radio. The result was the Grant, a squadron of which are seen here in the Western Desert. The sponson-mounted main armament and the height of the vehicle made it very difficult to fight the Lee and Grant from a hull-down position. (RAC Tank Museum)

steady improvement both in the pace and scope with which Soviet armoured operations were conducted, culminating in the destruction of the German Army Group Centre a year later during Operation 'Bagration'. Having thus overcome its own terrible inertia, the Soviet armoured corps rolled on to complete its victory in Eastern Europe and to defeat the Japanese Kwantung Army in Manchuria with a classic application of the *Blitzkrieg* technique. Yet, dramatic and decisive as these events were, it should also be remembered that during the same period the Wehrmacht was in steady decline, its own flexibility hamstrung by Hitler's orders to hold its ground at any price, and that the Japanese were simply not equipped to fight a mechanized war. On balance, therefore, it would not be unfair to suggest that when the guns fell silent in 1945 the Soviet armoured corps had become an extremely formidable force which had learned many lessons at a fearful price, but that at the tactical level its techniques still fell some way short of those of the German and Western armies.

One such technique which the universal possession of radio enabled Western tank crews to develop was that of indirect firing in the supplementary artillery role. This was employed during periods of comparatively static warfare in Italy, Normandy, north-west Europe and Burma and was used to drop harassing fire on distant targets. Because of the range involved, the target was invisible to the tank crew, but corrections based on the fall of shot (e.g., 'Right 50, Add 200') were signalled by an observer at the front. The gunner then adjusted his lay accordingly, using his traverse indicator and clinometer. Normally, only one tank was engaged in this ranging process but once the relevant coordinates had been established the rest of the tanks in the troop or squadron would join in the shoot.

This technique was ingeniously adapted for use in the Arakan, Burma, where the Japanese bunker complexes were located on jungle-covered hillsides, invisible to the tanks which were supplying the assaulting infantry with direct gunfire support from the valley below. A forward tank officer (FTO) was attached to the infantry and accompanied them during the attack. His first task was to direct the tanks' fire on to a feature which was visible to them, such as a prominent tree or a patch of scrub. Once this had been acquired it served as a datum point from which corrections could be made when the Japanese opened fire. The FTO would adjust the tanks' fall of shot until high-explosive shells had blown away the vegetation concealing the fire slit. The tanks would then switch to armour-piercing shot and smash up the bunker timbers; if possible, a smoke round was fired into the aperture, the smoke seeping along the galleries and indicating further fire slits. Once the FTO and the infantry's commanding officer were satisfied that the fire of the bunkers had been neutralized, the tanks would revert to HE and fire a rolling barrage ahead of the infantry as they assaulted the hill.

THE GUN/ ARMOUR SPIRAL

From 1939 to 1942 the tank was the weapon system that dominated the battlefields of Europe and North Africa. In 1939 the German panzer corps had crushed the gallant but largely unmechanized Polish Army in a classic application of *Vernichtungsgedanke* which employed a huge double-envelopment. The following year von Manstein's brilliant *Sichelschnitt* (Sickle-Cut) Plan resulted in the German armour driving a 40-mile-wide corridor through the French armies from the River Meuse to the Channel coast, trapping the best Allied troops, including the BEF, in a contracting pocket to the north from which the only escape lay across the Dunkirk beaches. The DLMs had fought well despite sustaining serious loss, but the DCRs, the most powerful armoured formations that France possessed, were quickly eliminated when they were committed in an unco-ordinated response to the German penetration. 1st DCR, engaged by Hoth's XV Panzer Corps and

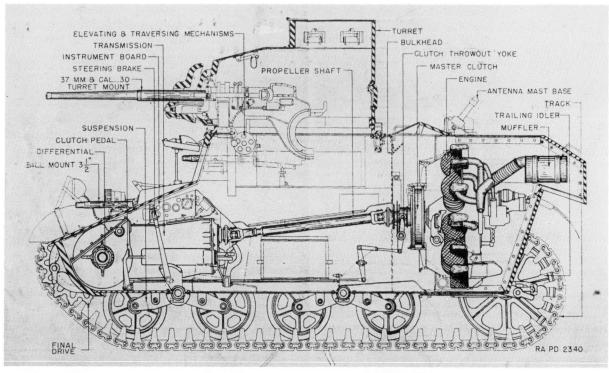

ELEVATING & TRAVERSING MECHANISMS
TRANSMISSION
INSTRUMENT BOARD
STEERING BRAKE
37 MM & CAL..30
TURRET MOUNT

SUSPENSION
CLUTCH PEDAL
DIFFERENTIAL
BALL MOUNT 3½"

PROPELLER SHAFT

TURRET
BULKHEAD
CLUTCH THROWOUT YOKE
MASTER CLUTCH
ENGINE
ANTENNA MAST BASE
TRACK
TRAILING IDLER
MUFFLER

FINAL
DRIVE

RA PD 2340

Left: Cross-section of a Stuart light tank taken from a Second World War manual. The thickness of the armour is depicted by the cross-hatching.

battered by the Luftwaffe, was bypassed and forced to withdraw, abandoning many of its vehicles for lack of fuel; 2nd DCR, fragmented by sloppy staff work, never re-formed as a division and was destroyed piecemeal; incredibly, 3rd DCR was initially deployed as a line of static pillboxes by a local corps commander, and then became bogged down in a mutually destructive battle of attrition; and weak attacks by De Gaulle's incomplete 4th DCR against the southern flank of the panzer corridor were easily contained. What might have been achieved was demonstrated by the slow infantry tanks of the British 1 Army Tank Brigade which counter-attacked near Arras on 21 May and for a while cut Major-General Erwin Rommel's 7th Panzer Division in two, generating such alarm that the German drive to the coast was temporarily suspended. While the Dunkirk evacuation was in progress the surviving French armies established a new line based on the Somme. This they fought hard to

hold, but having already lost the greater part of their armoured formations, they were unable to stem the German breakthrough when it came, and on 22 June France was forced to accept a humiliating armistice.

Italy had declared war on the United Kingdom and France on 10 June. The subsequent skirmishes in the Western Desert revealed that the Italian Army was neither physically nor mentally prepared for a mechanized war in a desert environment. Despite the poor showing of his troops, Mussolini insisted that they invade Egypt and in September an advance was made as far as Sidi Barrani. The heavily outnumbered British counter-attacked in December and in two months' fighting utterly destroyed an army of ten divisions, took 130,000 prisoners, captured 380 tanks and 845 guns, and advanced more than 500 miles at a cost of only 500 killed and 1,373 wounded. Throughout the short campaign the Italians had been hamstrung by the fact

Left: Vehicle maintenance on the tank park. In the foreground a Valentine's slack track is being taken up. The next vehicle is a Matilda, the 2pdr gun of which is being pulled through.

Right: The Valentine accounted for one-quarter of the United Kingdom's tank production, the majority being armed with the 2pdr gun. (IWM)

that if they attempted to fight a mobile battle they were routed by 7th Armoured Division, yet if they tried to fight from behind prepared defences, as at Sidi Barrani, Bardia and Tobruk, they were overrun by invulnerable Matildas which spearheaded the assault of aggressive Indian or Australian infantry. The defeat led directly to the dispatch of German assistance and resulted in a major campaign which would rage in the desert for the next two years.

Following the fall of France Hitler decided to double the number of his panzer divisions and achieved this by halving the tank strength of each. This actually produced a more balanced ratio between the tank and infantry elements of the division, and as the war progressed every major army would strive to achieve a similar balance. In April 1941 the Panzerwaffe overran Yugoslavia and Greece in a lightning campaign in which the difficult Balkan terrain created more difficulties than the enemy.

On 22 June 1941 Hitler launched his invasion of the Soviet Union under the code-name of Operation 'Barbarossa'. For this gigantic undertaking the German Army had available 3,332 tanks, but of

these only 965 were Pz Kpfw IIIs and 439 Pz Kpfw IVs; the balance was made up with light tanks or ageing Czech stock. For a while all went well. The Soviet Army, out-thought and out-fought, was carved into nine major and thirteen minor pockets which yielded more than three million prisoners and 26,000 guns. About 20,000 tanks were destroyed or abandoned and the Soviet capacity to prolong the war would have been eliminated altogether had not Stalin arranged for the tank production plants to be moved lock, stock and barrel far to the east. Notwithstanding the scale of these victories, 'Barbarossa' did not succeed. The arrival of the ferocious Russian winter coincided with that of tough Siberian reinforcement divisions. Moscow and Leningrad remained untaken and some of the captured ground was lost to counter-attacks. By December the Wehrmacht had shot its bolt, having itself incurred approximately 800,000 casualties and lost 2,300 tanks.

The reasons for the German failure included the comparatively late start induced by the need to mount the Balkan campaign, which restricted the amount of time available before the early winter rains turned roads into mud wallows in which

Above: Valentines in the Western Desert. The photograph suggests a recently arrived unit involved in an acclimatization exercise. The Bren anti-aircraft mounting was seldom fitted outside training; likewise, the rimmed steel helmet was worse than useless in the turret and would quickly be abandoned. (IWM)

Above: Crusader cruiser tanks and a Sherman being replenished by sea during the British Eighth Army's advance following the Second Battle of Alamein. (National Army Museum)

movement was impossible; Hitler's personal meddling in the conduct of operations, which cost yet more priceless time; and the unwillingness to recognize that since distances in Russia were infinitely greater than they had been in France the incidence of mechanical failure among the tanks would rise to critical proportions in the later stages of the offensive.

The Panzerwaffe would win fresh victories in Russia during 1942, but they would lead nowhere save to the encirclement of the German Sixth Army at Stalingrad, and for this the responsibility again rested with Adolf Hitler, who had personally assumed the responsibilities of Commander-in-Chief of the Army during the recriminations that followed 'Barbarossa'. In North Africa, too, the newly-created Field Marshal Rommel, having inflicted a severe defeat on the British armour at Gazala and captured Tobruk, had embarked on an ambitious advance into Egypt which over-extended his supply line to the extent that once his panzer divisions had been finally halted they lacked sufficient fuel either to advance or withdraw.

On the other side of the world the

Japanese Army had also passed the high point in its career of conquest. It had successfully used tanks in support of infantry operations in Malaya, Burma and the Philippines and although these were worsted in a number of engagements with Stuarts in Burma and Luzon, the numbers involved were comparatively small and the overall outcome so satisfactory that Japanese complacency remained undented. Even if the lessons of these isolated incidents had been taken to heart there was a limit to what could have been achieved before the Allies returned to the offensive in the Far Eastern theatre of war, particularly as the Imperial Navy's claims on steel production and skilled labour outweighed those of the armoured corps by a wide margin.

In the west, however, it became a matter of survival that armies should act upon the technical lessons demonstrated by the fighting thus far. In the main, these revolved around the ability of guns to penetrate armour plate and the converse aspect of the equation, the ability of armour plate to resist armour-piercing shot. The result became known as the Gun/Armour Spiral, which was maintained throughout the war as each side installed more powerful guns and was in turn forced to employ thicker armour as a defence against those of the enemy. Larger guns required larger turrets and wider turret rings, and this meant that hulls had to be correspondingly bigger. These developments, coupled with the fitting of thicker armour, resulted in an increase in weight with which only a stronger suspension system and more powerful engine could cope. Obviously, some tanks had little or no potential for up-gunning and up-armouring and when what there was had been exhausted it became necessary to design a replacement. Thus, the tanks of 1945 bore only a passing family resemblance to those of 1939.

The Gun/Armour Spiral began modestly enough with a general recognition that the light tank had a very limited role on the modern battlefield. The British family of light tanks was withdrawn in 1941 although the American Stuart was extensively used in the Western Desert and in fact remained in service with the Allied armies from 1941 until the war ended. The German Army was forced to retain its light tanks to fill out the ranks of its panzer divisions, but after the failure of 'Barbarossa' those that survived were withdrawn and their chassis converted to other uses. In the Soviet Army, which continued to develop this class of vehicle for a while, the T-34 eventually absorbed the duties of the light tank and performed them more efficiently.

Encounters with the French Char B and the British Matilda during the 1940 battles had revealed the inadequacy of the 37mm gun mounted by the Pz Kpfw III. Hitler therefore issued instructions that the tank was to be up-gunned with a 50mm weapon, thereby absorbing the spare capacity which, it will be recalled, had been allowed during the design phase. He had specified that the 50mm L/60 gun (i.e., with a length of 50mm x 60) was to be fitted, but partly because of supply difficulties the shorter, and therefore less powerful, 50mm L/42 version was used. The discovery that he had been deceived resulted in one of his unbridled rages, during which he unfairly castigated the Pz Kpfw III as a poor design,

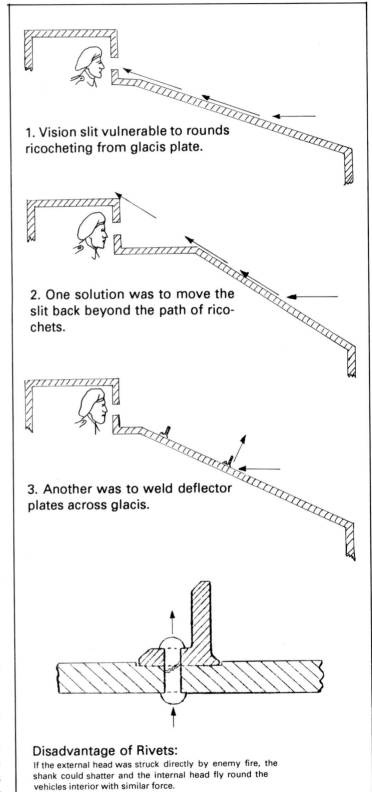

1. Vision slit vulnerable to rounds ricocheting from glacis plate.

2. One solution was to move the slit back beyond the path of ricochets.

3. Another was to weld deflector plates across glacis.

Disadvantage of Rivets:
If the external head was struck directly by enemy fire, the shank could shatter and the internal head fly round the vehicles interior with similar force.

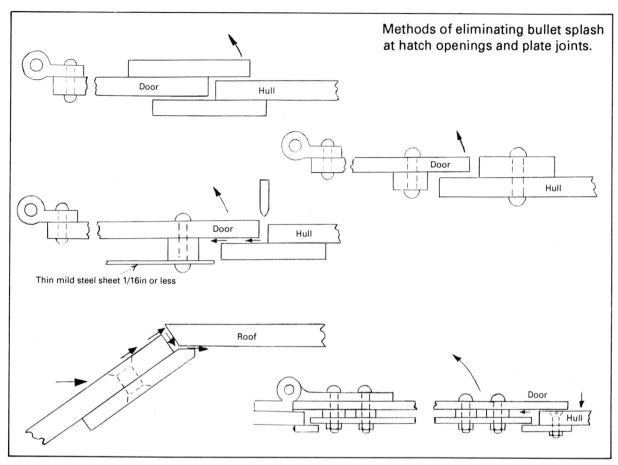

Methods of eliminating bullet splash at hatch openings and plate joints.

Door

Hull

Door

Hull

Door

Hull

Thin mild steel sheet 1/16in or less

Roof

Door

Hull

Right: Pz Kpfw III Model J, armed with the 50mm L/60 gun. (Charles K. Kliment)

Left: Loader's view of the main and coaxial armament of a Pz Kpfw III. In this case the main armament is the 50mm L/42 gun, which was muzzle-heavy in its mounting and counter-balanced by a small ingot on the back of the spent case deflector shield. The longer 50mm L/60 gun was balanced by a compression spring in a cylinder to the right of the mounting. (IWM)

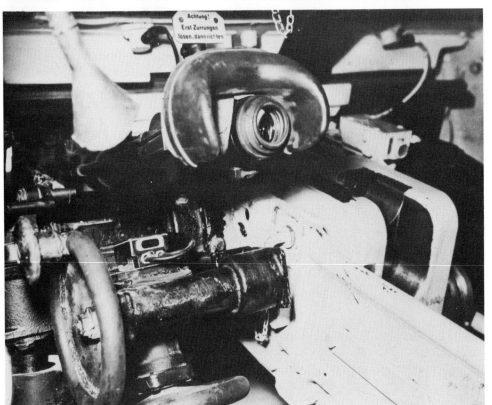

Left: Pz Kpfw III gun control equipment showing elevation and traverse handwheels, gunsight with browpad and the voice tube linking the gunner and commander. (IWM)

and the L/60 weapon was promptly fitted, reaching regiments at the end of 1941. This, however, represented the limit of the Pz Kpfw III's capacity. The 50mm L/60 was muzzle-heavy in its mounting and to compensate this a small compression spring housed in a cylinder was mounted on the turret ring and attached to the gun. Similar devices employing compression spring, hydraulic or hydro-pneumatic cylinders were also installed in the up-gunned versions of the Pz Kpfw IV, the Panther and the Tigers to counter the muzzle-heaviness of their main armament.

The tempo of the Gun/Armour Spiral accelerated dramatically following the first encounters with the KV and the T-34. The Panzerwaffe's confidence was seriously jolted by the discovery that not only could its 37mm and short 50mm guns make little impression on the armour of these Soviet tanks, but also that the latter's 76.2mm armament was capable of out-ranging and defeating every German tank in service. Up-gunning the Pz Kpfw III to 50mm L/60 standard was far from being a complete

answer, but as the Pz Kpfw IV also possessed a wide turret ring it was possible to replace its 75mm L/24 howitzer with a high velocity 75mm L/43 gun which had a muzzle velocity of 2,428 feet per second and could penetrate 89mm armour set back at 30 degrees. This began entering service early in 1942 and was replaced the following year by an improved 75mm L/48 gun. Both these weapons were also fitted to the Sturmartillerie's assault guns and, as described elsewhere, large numbers of obsolete light tank chassis were converted to the tank destroyer role by mounting 75mm anti-tank guns. In the longer term only the production of a new medium tank would suffice and the basic specification for this, the Pz Kpfw V, better known as the Panther, was issued as early as November 1941. The Panther, armed with a 75mm L/70 gun, was rushed through its development phase and entered service in the summer of 1943. Simultaneously, and somewhat outside the mainstream of the Panzerwaffe's operational concepts, work had been continuing on a heavily-

Below: The Pz Kpfw IV's turret ring was wide enough for the vehicle to be up-gunned and during the war's latter years it equipped one battalion in each panzer regiment, armed with a 75mm L/48 gun. (RAC Tank Museum)

Left: Close-support version of the Cromwell cruiser tank, armed with a 95mm howitzer. (RAC Tank Museum)

armoured 54-ton breakthrough tank armed with an 88mm L/56 gun which was capable of destroying any tank in the world. This, the Pz Kpfw VI or Tiger E, was issued to independent heavy tank battalions and had its baptism of fire on the Leningrad sector in August 1942. Hardly had the Tiger E entered service than German designers were instructed to produce an even more powerful version which would break the cycle and give the Panzerwaffe a decisive technical lead. The result was the 69-ton Tiger B, armed with an 88mm L/71 gun, which began leaving the production lines in February 1944.

For their part the Russians increased the

calibre-length of the 76.2mm guns mounted by the KV and T-34 from L/30.5 to L/41.2, but by 1943 they had lost their qualitative advantage. As an interim measure pending the development of a new heavy tank the KV was up-gunned with an 85mm L/53 weapon. The same weapon was chosen to up-gun the T-34, although this required a completely re-designed three-man turret. This vehicle, designated T-34/85 while the earlier models became known as T-34/76, began reaching the front in the spring of 1944. Meanwhile, the IS (Iosef Stalin) series of heavy tanks had been developed from the KV and were also leaving the factories. The

Left: Cromwells of the 2nd Welsh Guards advance across open country near Escoville, July 1944. 2nd Welsh Guards was the armoured reconnaissance regiment of the Guards Armoured Division. (RAC Tank Museum)

Right: Interior of KV1 turret showing breech of 76.2mm main armament, elevation and traverse handwheels, gunsight and episcopes. The 7.62mm coaxial machine-gun can be seen to the right of the main armament with its drum magazine fitted and several more magazines in the rack above. (IWM)

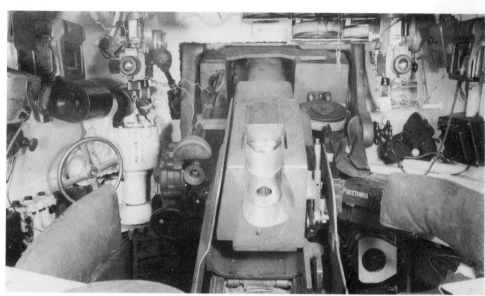

Left: M3A3 Stuarts being handed over to the Yugoslav 1st Partisan Tank Brigade at Bari, Italy, 1944–5. (IWM)

Right: Rear interior face of KV1 turret showing machine-gun mounting and the method of stowing ready-use ammunition. (IWM)

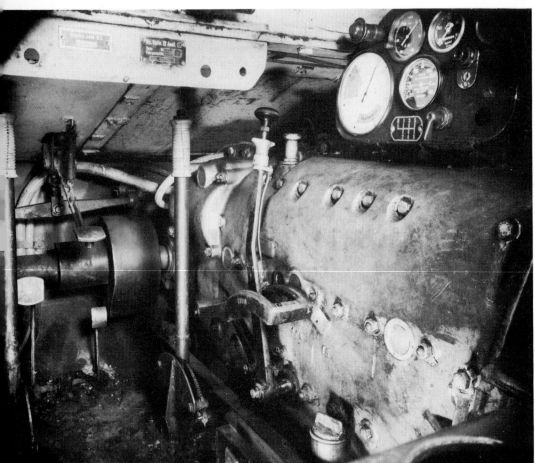

Above: Replacing the Chrysler Multibank power unit of a South African Sherman M4A4, Florence 1944. (South African National Museum of Military History)

Left: Pz Kpfw IV driver's controls and instrument panel. (IWM)

Above: The Russian IS-II heavy tank.

IS-II was armed with a 122mm L/43 gun with a muzzle velocity of 2,562 feet per second, and although this was less than the German 88mm L/56 (2,657fps) and 88mm L/71 (3,340fps) it relied on the mass of its round as much as velocity for its effect and was capable of penetrating 185mm of armour at 1,000 yards. The IS-II was regarded as being more than a match for the up-gunned Pz Kpfw IV and the Panther, but could be penetrated by the Tiger E at 1,900 yards.

In the Western Desert the effects of the Gun/Armour Spiral were less dramatic. The British had been on the point of introducing the 6pdr tank gun during 1940 but the loss of so much equipment in France, the threat of invasion and the need to defend Egypt meant that, of sheer necessity, factories had to keep producing the 2pdr until they could find time to re-tool. Thus, until the summer of 1942 they were forced to rely on the 2pdr, supplemented by the 37mm of the Stuart, which had a similar performance. An uneasy feeling developed among British tank crews that they were out-gunned, and

this was to persist throughout the campaign, although it was not altogether justified. The 2pdr was, in fact, a slightly better weapon than the German 37mm and achieved approximate parity with the 50mm L/42. The Africa Corps received its first 50mm L/60 Pz Kpfw IIIs in time for the great tank battle at Gazala, but on this occasion it was the British, with their 75mm Grants, who had a clear qualitative advantage. During the Second Battle of Alamein the small number of 75mm L/43 Pz Kpfw IVs present were the most powerful tanks possessed by either side, although they could not hope to prevail against the Eighth Army's infinitely more numerous Shermans. A handful of Tigers reached Tunisia, providing Allied crews and design teams alike with ample food for thought, but again, they were too few to affect the outcome. Subsequent analysis of the campaign revealed that British tank losses arose not simply from tank v. tank engagements but rather more from the German 'sword-and-shield' tactics which involved the aggressive use of anti-tank guns, notably the legendary 88mm dual-

purpose anti-aircraft/anti-tank gun and the 50mm, PaK 38.

It was during the 18-month period that followed the end of the North African campaign that the Western Allies were regularly out-gunned by German tanks which had been designed with the requirements of the Eastern Front in mind. The British never quite recovered the ground they had lost earlier in the war, the 6pdr being overtaken by events, as was the 75mm L/40 gun mounted by the Cromwell and the Churchill VII, which had a similar performance to that of the Sherman. The 76.2mm L/58.4 17pdr, introduced in 1944, was an excellent weapon which achieved parity with the Panther and armed the Sherman Firefly, the Centurion prototype and several tank destroyers, but there were never enough to go round. A shorter (L/50) version of the gun, designated the 77mm, was fitted to the Comet Cruiser tank. The Americans, too, developed more powerful AFV armaments, including the 76mm L/55 which armed some of the later models of the Sherman, and the M-18 tank destroyer; and the 90mm L/53 mounted by the M-26 Pershing heavy tank and the M-36 tank destroyer, which was capable of penetrating the Tiger E.

Left: Valentine Mark IX, armed with a 6pdr gun.

Below: The Comet was the last of the British cruiser series to employ the Christie suspension.

In 1939 medium and cruiser tanks had gone to war protected by frontal armour which averaged 30mm, while for heavy and infantry tanks 78mm was regarded as impressive. By 1945, however, the situation had altered dramatically. The Panther had 80mm frontal armour with 120mm on the mantlet; the T-34/85 75mm; the Sherman 105mm; and the Comet 101mm. In the heavy class the Tiger E had 110mm armour and the Tiger B 185mm; the IS-II 160mm; the M-26 Pershing 110mm; and the Churchill VII 152mm. In the majority of cases designers had increased the

protection factor by presenting a sloped glacis to the enemy's shot, the most notable exceptions being the Tiger E and the Churchill, which betrayed their pre-war origins with their vertical plates and reliance on mass alone for their defence.

Throughout the Second World War the principal means of penetrating armour remained kinetic energy, i.e., a solid shot fired at high velocity which would bore its way through the protective plate and into the tank's interior. The basic armour-piercing (AP) shot was made from steel alloy, but this was found to break up on impact with face-hardened plate. To prevent this a cap was fitted and the round became known as armour-piercing capped (APC). Further development included the addition of a ballistic cap to improve streamlining in flight, this type of ammunition being designated armour-piercing capped (ballistic cap) (APCBC). In 1941 the Germans began using the armour-piercing composite rigid (APCR) round. This employed an extremely hard tungsten carbide core surrounded by a soft metal jacket which applied 'squeeze' to the shot and therefore produced a higher muzzle velocity, making penetration by the sub-calibre core much easier. The major disadvantage with this type of shot was that since it was lighter than the normal AP projectile yet retained the same diameter its velocity and penetrative power decreased rapidly with range. None the less, this type of ammunition was adopted by the Russians in 1942 and by the Americans two years later.

In 1944 the British introduced an armour-piercing discarding sabot (APDS) round for use by the 6pdr marks of Churchill. In this case the tungsten carbide core was surrounded by a soft jacket or sabot which applied 'squeeze' while the round was travelling up the barrel but fell off on leaving the muzzle, the effect being to accelerate the core. The performance of the APDS round fell away less rapidly than that of the APCR and at ranges up to 2,000 yards it achieved as much as 50 per cent better penetration than the equivalent APCBC projectile.

A second means of penetrating armour plate began reaching the battlefield in 1942. This relied on chemical rather than kinetic energy and was originally known as the Monro Effect, the principles of which were used to develop hollow-charge ammunition. In simple terms this consists of a cylinder of high-explosive that has a conical cavity lined with copper at one end. On detonation the whole force of the explosion is focused in an immensely powerful narrow jet which reaches velocities of up to 30,000 feet per second and is capable of blasting a hole through the thickest armour. Ammunition of this type does not require a high-velocity gun to achieve its effect and is very suitable for use as an infantry anti-tank weapon. During the second half of the war the issue of such hollow-charge ammunition projectors as the British PIAT, the American Bazooka and the German *Panzerfaust* gave the infantry an ability to defeat armour at close quarters that they had previously lacked, and was an important factor in ending the tank's era of total domination. The only effective defence that the tank could offer was so-called spaced armour in the form of sheet-metal skirting plates, turret girdles and external stowage bins against which the round would burst, the worst effects of the explosion being dispersed before they reached the main armour. The name generally used for this type of ammunition when fired by tank or anti-tank guns is HEAT (high-explosive anti-tank). It was widely used by the Germans in AFVs mounting the 75mm L/43 and 75mm L/48, the 88mm L/56 and 88mm L/71, in which it supplemented the supply of APCR ammunition, and by the British for the 95mm L/26 howitzer which armed the close support tanks Centaur, Cromwell IV and VI, and Churchill V and VIII.

In addition to firing armour-defeating rounds, the majority of tank guns also fired conventional high-explosive (HE) shells and smoke rounds, important exceptions being the British 2pdr and 6pdr, for which HE ammunition was not available during the first half of the war. The American 37mm gun which armed the Stuart series and the top turret of the Lee/Grant also fired an anti-personnel canister round for which the principal application lay in close-quarter fighting against the Japanese. Types of machine-gun ammunition in use included ball, tracer, AP and incendiary, these generally being loaded in a standard belt-mix which could be altered as the situation demanded. As the war continued it became apparent that the contribution made by the hull or bow machine-gun was very limited, the space occupied by the hull gunner being sometimes used to stow more main armament ammunition.

Gunsight telescopes could be periscopic, but were normally direct-vision and penetrated the mantlet coaxially with the main armament. The sight picture included range scales for the various types of ammunition, i.e., AP, HE, smoke and coaxial machine-gun, together with a graticule pattern incorporating aim-off marks which the gunner would lay on to the target, using power traverse to obtain general direction and then his traverse and elevation handwheels for his final lay. German sighting telescopes were slightly more complicated and incorporated two movable transparent plates. The first or range plate rotated about its own axis, the main and coaxial armament range scales being marked on opposite quadrants. The second or sighting plate moved in a vertical plane and contained the sighting and aim-off marks. The two plates moved simultaneously, the sighting plate rising

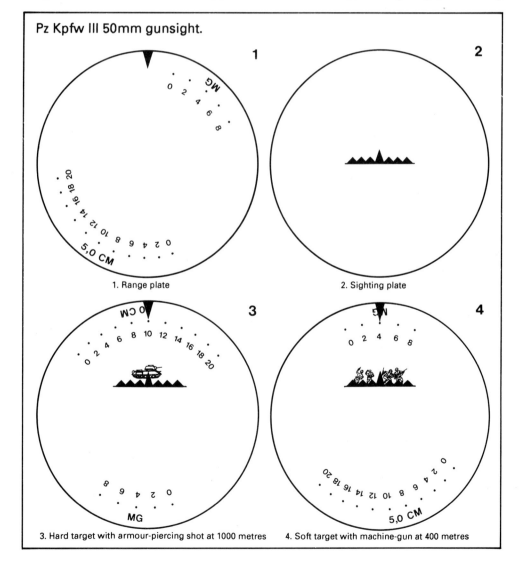

Pz Kpfw III 50mm gunsight.

1. Range plate

2. Sighting plate

3. Hard target with armour-piercing shot at 1000 metres

4. Soft target with machine-gun at 400 metres

and falling as the range plate turned. To engage at the selected range, the range wheel was turned until the appropriate figure was opposite a pointer at the top of the sight, and the sighting mark was laid on to the target by the traverse and elevation controls. The system was efficient but took a little longer to operate.

During this period all ranges had to be estimated unless they were previously known and although every gunner sought to achieve a first-round hit this was not always possible. The burning trace in the base of the round would tell the gunner where his shot had gone and he would correct his lay, first for line then for elevation. If, for example, his first round had fallen short of the target he would apply a standard correction and if the next round fell beyond it he would halve the correction and strike with the third round. With experience, the drill could be reduced to two rounds. Although modern tanks are fitted with extremely sophisticated fire control computers which provide exact ranges and other ballistic data, virtually guaranteeing a first-round hit, the technique is still taught in case of malfunction.

In pre-war days much emphasis had been placed on firing on the move. The realities of the battlefield soon showed this to be a waste of time and ammunition as far as accuracy was concerned, but it could be used to good moral effect when breaking into or through an enemy position. An elevation stabilizer was fitted to the Sherman's 75mm gun, with disappointing results. Full stabilization in elevation and azimuth was not achieved until 1949, when it was installed in the Centurion III; even then, careful timing was required if anything like satisfactory results were to be obtained. During the Second World War only firing at the halt offered a reasonable chance of successfully concluding an engagement.

Nevertheless, there was a considerable advance in the techniques of semi-indirect and indirect firing, using the tank's traverse indicator and clinometer. In the former the target is concealed from the gunner by a feature such as a crest and he applies the

corrections given him by the commander, who has the target and the fall of shot in view from his position in the cupola. In the latter (which will be dealt with more fully in the next section) the target is invisible to both gunner and commander and the corrections are received by radio from a distant observer. Both techniques were used during periods of static warfare in Italy and on the Western Front when tanks were required to perform the role of supplementary artillery or put down intermittent harassing fire on distant objectives such as crossroads.

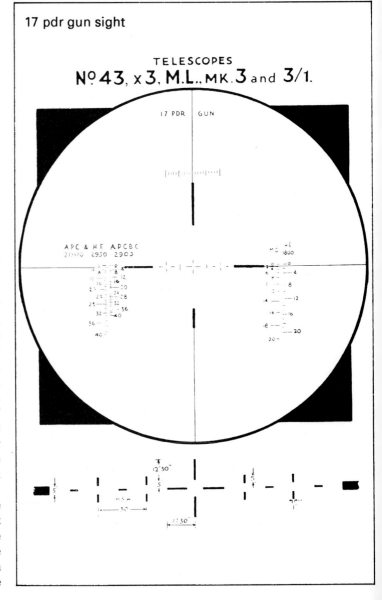

17 pdr gun sight

THE TANK'S PARTNERS

The armoured car had a longer ancestry than the tank and was used by most armies for a variety of duties including raids, convoy escort, internal security and liaison, although its widest application was in the reconnaissance role. Armoured cars were relatively simple to construct, and indeed many designs were based on commercial vehicle chassis, although as the war progressed purpose-built chassis were also introduced. Armament, too, was steadily improved, but when engaged in reconnaissance the car's most important weapon was its radio, which was used to report the enemy's presence or otherwise, his strength and dispositions, his activities, or to call down an artillery or air strike.

The German Army's concept of armoured operations involved reconnaissance in depth, with reconnaissance elements operating up to twenty miles ahead of the main body of the panzer division. For this reason the division's armoured reconnaissance battalion had a large establishment which included two armoured reconnaissance squadrons with armoured cars, a motor-cycle machine-gun squadron, and a heavy weapons squadron with light artillery, anti-tank gun and assault pioneer troops, the motor-cycle machine-gun and heavy weapons squadrons being used to punch a hole in the opposing line through which the armoured cars would pass into the enemy's hinterland. While the nature of the armoured reconnaissance battalion's work remained unaltered throughout the war, operational experience resulted in a number of organizational changes. The motor-cycle element sustained heavy casualties and was gradually phased out, and, as a result of the atrocious going on the Eastern Front, particularly in the spring and autumn mud, Sd Kfz 250 series halftracks in

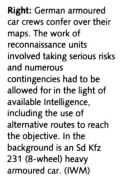

Right: German armoured car crews confer over their maps. The work of reconnaissance units involved taking serious risks and numerous contingencies had to be allowed for in the light of available Intelligence, including the use of alternative routes to reach the objective. In the background is an Sd Kfz 231 (8-wheel) heavy armoured car. (IWM)

their various forms undertook most of the battalion's duties, although one squadron retained its armoured cars.

British and American armoured divisions also contained an armoured reconnaissance unit. The British armoured car regiment consisted of three armoured car squadrons, each containing a squadron headquarters troop and three armoured car troops; latterly, squadron organization varied somewhat between theatres and might include a heavy troop with M3 75mm tank destroyers and an assault troop, carried in halftracks. The American armoured cavalry reconnaissance squadron was a battalion-sized unit which consisted of three reconnaissance troops (squadrons) each containing a troop headquarters and three platoons, equipped

with M8 armoured cars; a light tank company of three platoons; and an assault gun troop (squadron) of four platoons, equipped with a total of eight light self-propelled howitzers.

In the Western Desert British and Commonwealth armoured car units operated well in advance of their parent formations, but during the periods of static warfare in Italy and Western Europe their activities were inevitably confined. Whenever the German front collapsed Allied cars came into their own again and numerous instances are recorded where their probes detected an undefended bridge or route forward which was quickly exploited by their divisional commanders. The same was true in Burma where, once the Japanese had been driven out of

Left: Detail of 20mm cannon mounting and anti-grenade grilles of an Sd Kfz 222 light armoured car. (RAC Tank Museum)

Right: Daimler armoured cars of the 11th Hussars. The regiment fired the first shots of the North African war in 1940 and during the next three years its badgeless brown beret became known throughout the desert by friend and foe alike. (IWM)

Mandalay, armoured cars formed part of the Fourteenth Army's fast-moving advance guard during its 300-mile dash to Rangoon. On the Eastern Front the Soviet Army had lost most of its obsolete armoured car fleet by the end of 1941 and thereafter its ground reconnaissance was carried out by light tanks, motor-cycle patrols or mounted cavalry units.

By 1939 it was universally accepted that armoured formations must contain their own organic infantry units if they were to succeed in their tasks. The functions of the infantry included holding the ground which the tanks had captured; protecting the shoulders of a salient driven through the enemy line; flank protection of the divisional axis of advance; dealing with anti-tank guns in local situations; protecting the tanks in night laagers; securing river crossing sites; house-clearing in built-up areas; and reducing pockets of resistance, to name but a few. At first, every army made the mistake of including too high a proportion of tanks to infantry within its armoured divisions with the result that the latter were overworked beyond the point of efficiency, but by 1942 a state of balance had been restored by reducing the number of tank battalions within the division while the infantry element remained constant.

It was also universally accepted that the infantry serving within the armoured division must have a mobility comparable to that of the tanks, although the need for protection was less generally acknowledged and comparatively little progress had been made in the development of the armoured personnel carrier (APC). The world's first purpose-built APC was the British Tank Mk IX, which was produced just too late to see action in 1918. In this sphere the most important event in the years following the First World War was the partnership established between Adolphe Kegresse, who had formerly managed the Tsar's garage where he had produced a half-track system suitable for movement across snow, and the French Citroen company. In 1923 five Citroen-Kegresse halftracks successfully completed the first motorized crossing of the Sahara, the system being subsequently adopted by the French Army as the basis of a series of weapon and personnel carriers for the *Dragons Portées* which formed the rifle element of the newly mechanized cavalry divisions. The future of the halftrack was now assured. Fitted with splinter- and bullet-proof armour, it was to dominate mechanized infantry operations throughout the Second War, since it was the only type of personnel carrier that could keep pace with tanks when moving across country.

Left: Staghound armoured cars of the 2nd New Zealand Divisional Cavalry Regiment, Italy, November 1943. (New Zealand Official)

Right: An Sd Kfz 251 halftrack APC, with air recognition flag draped across its bonnet, leaves a German-occupied fort in the Western Desert. The traffic-control disc suggests that its passengers belong to a Feldgendarmerie unit. (RAC Tank Museum)

Curiously, it was adopted for general service only by the German and United States armies, and then only after a protracted development history involving, in both cases, experimental artillery prime movers. The German Sd Kfz 251 armoured halftrack was an excellent APC but it remained in chronically short supply. In May 1940, on the eve of the great German offensive in the west, only two of the army's eighty battalions of motorized infantry were equipped with APCs. By September 1943 there were 226 motorized infantry battalions, but only sufficient APCs for 26 of these; the remainder had to make do with unarmoured versions of the vehicle or lorries. This situation was aggravated by the diversion of APCs for other uses. There were no less than twenty variants of the basic Sd Kfz 251 and a dozen or so of the smaller Sd Kfz 250, including weapons carriers, command vehicles, engineer vehicles, armoured ambulances, and so on. Some of these were undoubtedly useful,

but others were an expensive luxury. Initially, the motor rifle element of the panzer division had also included a motor-cycle battalion, but by the time 'Barbarossa' had run its course this had sustained such serious casualties that it was broken up and its survivors posted to the armoured reconaissance battalion. On 5 July 1942 the panzer divisions' motor rifle troops were honoured by Hitler with the prestigious title of Panzergrenadier, this being extended to motorized divisions the following March.

In the United States the M2 and M3 half-track series went into mass production and were used not only to equip the armoured infantry battalions of the armoured divisions, but also formed the basis of a large number of self-propelled fire-support, anti-tank and anti-aircraft weapon systems. These were followed by the similar M5 and M9 halftrack series, most of which were supplied to America's allies.

The British Army developed a series of light, fully tracked vehicles, referred to as

Right: On the Eastern Front severe winter conditions and the mud induced by autumn rain and the spring thaw inhibited the use of armoured cars to such an extent that German armoured reconnaissance battalions were additionally equipped with Sd Kfz 250 halftracks, which were capable of operating where the wheeled vehicles could not. (RAC Tank Museum)

Bren or Universal weapons carriers, that were employed in a wide variety of roles throughout the war. The motorized infantry battalions forming part of the Commonwealth and Polish armoured divisions rode in 15-cwt lorries, but when American halftracks began arriving in the middle of 1943 these were progressively phased out. For infantry units that did not possess their own organic APCs the British and Canadians developed the Kangaroo, a turretless Sherman or Ram tank in which an infantry section rode in what had been the fighting compartment. In north-west Europe the 79th Armoured Division possessed two Kangaroo APC regiments which were allocated to infantry formations as operational requirements demanded. Another variation on this theme was the Unfrocked Priest, which was capable of carrying two infantry sections, and consisted of the Howitzer Motor Carriage M7 (Priest) with the main armament removed. Most Unfrocked Priests served in a specially raised APC regiment on the Eighth Army sector of the Italian front, but a number were used by the Canadians in

their advance on Falaise during the Normandy campaign.

The Soviet Army's failure to develop an APC was a major factor in the terrible casualties it sustained. Whenever the Soviets attacked, the Germans were able to separate the tanks from their unprotected infantry by artillery fire, and since neither was then able to support the other's operations both suffered accordingly. In the long term it would have been less expensive in lives and equipment if a proportion of T-34 and light tank chassis production had been used in the Kangaroo role, but it was not to be, and those American halftracks that reached Russia as Lend-Lease aid tended to be retained by armoured formation headquarters.

The question of whether armoured infantry attacks should be made mounted or dismounted hinged entirely on the prevailing circumstances. If the defenders of the objective showed obvious signs of collapsing, giving up or bolting, a mounted attack in APCs could be pressed home. On the other hand, a mounted attack against a resolute defence was an extremely

Below: The Kangaroo was a turretless Canadian Ram medium tank capable of carrying an infantry section in the fighting compartment. In Italy a number of Shermans were also converted to this role. (RAC Tank Museum)

Right: The M3 halftrack APC was employed by American armoured infantry units and was also supplied to Allied armies. (RAC Tank Museum)

Below: Another variation on the Kangaroo theme was the 'Unfrocked Priest', which was a Howitzer Motor Carriage M7 stripped off its armament. This example has been fitted with a deep-wading exhaust. (RAC Tank Museum)

dangerous business, since much of the infantry's fire, delivered from inside a moving vehicle, was inevitably wasted, while the APCs themselves remained at high risk; the failed panzergrenadier attacks against the 2nd Battalion, the Parachute Regiment, holding the northern end of the Arnhem road-bridge, illustrate the point perfectly. In such circumstances, higher authority might agree to the objective being masked or bypassed, but if not a set-piece dismounted attack would be made with tank and artillery support.

Although self-propelled artillery weapons had been designed and used during the First World War and subsequently, the artillery of the world's armoured formations entered the Second World War with its guns towed by prime movers. This did not matter too much in western European countries with a well-developed road network, but in Poland, the Soviet Union and the Western Desert there were often nothing but poor, good-weather roads or no roads at all, and this meant that the artillery was sometimes physically incapable of keeping up with the tanks. Clearly, only a fully tracked chassis could be expected to confer comparable mobility and by 1942

most armies were well on their way to solving the problem by mounting guns on adapted tank chassis and surrounding them with a box of bullet- and splinter-proof armour plate.

In this respect the German Army was fortunate in that the 1941 fighting in the Soviet Union had confirmed the obsolescence of its light tank family and there were therefore plenty of chassis immediately available. The chassis of the Pz Kpfw II was fitted with a light 105mm howitzer, the conversion being known as the Wespe (wasp). Also available were a large number of French tanks captured in 1940, and because the design of these rendered them unsuitable for use with German first-line tank units, many of their chassis were similarly converted. The 105mm self-propelled howitzers served with the light batteries of the panzer divisions' artillery regiment from 1942 onwards. The medium battery of the regiment had to wait until 1943 for its Hummel (bumble-bee) 150mm self-propelled howitzers, which employed the larger Pz Kpfw IV chassis incorporating the final drive of the Pz Kpfw III. The heavy infantry gun companies of the panzer-

Left: Wespe 105mm self-propelled howitzer of an SS panzer division on the Eastern Front. The camouflage net has been cleverly stowed so that it can be rolled quickly fore and aft to cover the vehicle once the battery position has been established. (US National Archives)

Above: The Bishop 25pdr self-propelled gun/howitzer was based on the chassis of the Valentine infantry tank and often supplemented its on-board ammunition by towing a standard limber. (IWM)

grenadier regiments also received self-propelled mountings for its 150mm direct gunfire support weapons. The first of these, based on the Pz Kpfw I chassis, had actually seen active service in 1939 and 1940, but was top-heavy and performed badly across country. A much lower version, based on the Pz Kpfw II appeared in 1942 and was followed by two distinct models based on the Pz Kpfw 38(t), with the engine at the front and rear respectively.

The first modern British self-propelled field artillery weapon system to see active service was based on the Valentine tank chassis and armed with a 25pdr gun/howitzer housed in a tall fixed turret. It was not a success, partly because the limited elevation available (+15 degrees) restricted the maximum range to 6,400 yards as opposed to the towed 25pdr's 13,500 yards, partly because it carried only 32 rounds (although this was often remedied by towing a limber), and partly

because the parent chassis was itself slow at 15mph, and the overloaded conversion even slower. The vehicle reached North Africa in time to participate in the Second Battle of Alamein, where it provided support for 23 Armoured Brigade, an infantry tank formation, but was withdrawn from first-line service at the end of the Sicilian campaign. It was known universally at the time as the Valentine SP, but it is generally referred to as the Bishop, despite the probability that this name was conferred retrospectively. Also present at Second Alamein and serving with the artillery regiments of the armoured divisions was the American 105mm Howitzer Motor Carriage M7, which became known as the Priest in British service because of the distinctive pulpit mounting of its anti-aircraft machine-gun. The early models of the M7 were based on the chassis of the M3 Lee medium tank, but later models employed the M4A3 Sherman

Above: The 105mm Howitzer Motor Carriage M7 first saw action with the Eighth Army during the Second Battle of Alamein. In British service it became known as The Priest because of the AA machine-gun's pulpit mounting. The vehicle shown here carries the charging rhino insignia of 1st Armoured Division, the unit tactical number and, on the side, the battery marking. As part of the deception plan prior to the battle many AFVs were fitted with dummy lorry canopies and cabs and the rails which supported these were subsequently used by the crews to stow their packs, bedding and bivouac sheets. (IWM)

Left: Sexton self-propelled 25pdr gun/howitzer, based on the chassis of the Canadian Ram medium tank. (RAC Tank Museum)

medium tank chassis and were designated M7B1. From the middle of 1944 onwards British and Commonwealth armoured formations in north-west Europe and Italy began replacing their M7s with the Sexton, which was similar in appearance and layout, but consisted of a marriage between the chassis of the Canadian Ram medium tank and the 25pdr gun/howitzer, although M7s continued to serve in Burma until the end of the war. Many discarded M7s were employed in the Kangaroo APC role, as mentioned above.

Following the disastrous battle at Gazala and the fall of Tobruk, many American armoured artillery units had been stripped of their M7s, which had been dispatched to the hard-pressed British Eighth Army in Egypt. As a result of this, when they landed in North Africa in November 1942 they were temporarily equipped with the substitute-standard T19 105mm Howitzer Motor Carriage, which was based on the

M3 halftrack chassis. Fortunately, American industry saw to it that M7 production was accelerated and this remained the US armoured divisions' standard field artillery self-propelled mounting throughout the war, although in 1945 it was itself declared substitute-standard and was to have been replaced by the roomier M37 105mm Howitzer Motor Carriage, which employed the chassis of the M24 Chaffee light tank. The US Army also developed a number of self-propelled mountings for medium and heavy artillery weapons, the most important of these being the 155mm Gun Motor Carriage M12, consisting of a First World War gun mounted on an adapted M3 medium tank chassis, which saw active service in Europe. A widened M4A3 medium tank chassis was used for the improved M40 155mm Gun Motor Carriage and the M43 8in Howitzer Motor Carriage, but only a few of the former had reached the front when the war ended. Also overtaken by events were the M41 155mm Howitzer Motor Carriage and the T92 240mm Howitzer Motor Carriage, which employed respectively the chassis of the M24 Chaffee light tank and the M26 Pershing heavy tank; the T92 had been designed specifically for bunker-busting during the invasion of Japan.

The Soviet Army, as we have seen, was inherently less flexible than those of the West or Germany, and supported its armoured operations with pre-planned artillery programmes, often involving hundreds of towed guns firing wheel-to-wheel. Naturally, the Russians would have welcomed the same flexible artillery reaction which armoured formation commanders elsewhere could obtain in immediate response to a radio transmission, but with their limited resources this was simply not possible. Instead, they were forced to rely to a greater extent on direct gunfire support from their assault guns and tank destroyers. The only vehicle which came close to resembling a Western or German self-propelled artillery weapon was the SU-76, which combined a 76.2mm gun with the chassis of a T70 light tank, but even this was intended for open-sights firing.

Other armies made little or no use of self-propelled artillery, although the Italians adapted their M43 tank chassis as a fully tracked carriage for their Model 1935 149mm gun/howitzer. The problem with this equipment, which entered service shortly before Italy obtained an armistice from the Western Allies, was that it was simply a gun carriage manned by a driver and co-driver; no provision was made for the rest of the gun crew, nor for ammunition. Nevertheless, it remained in service throughout the Italian campaign and equipped several Fascist and German units.

The fluid nature of the fighting during the early years of the war meant that comparatively little attention was paid to the assault engineering aspects of armoured warfare, with the exception of a few bridgelaying, demolition and flame-throwing devices. In 1940, however, the German Army realized that if it wished to invade Britain it would have to give some thought to the problem of getting tanks ashore with the assault infantry, who would remain vulnerable until the strongpoints in the immediate vicinity had been subdued. It was decided, therefore, that the Pz Kpfw II would be fitted with flotation tanks and a propeller driven by an extension shaft from the engine, and swim ashore after launching itself from its invasion barge. Simultaneously, heavier Pz Kpfw IIIs and IVs, having been sealed with waterproof compound and rubber sheeting, were to launch themselves from their barges and drive ashore on the sea bed, air being supplied to the engine by a flexible 18-metre hose which was held on the surface by a buoy, while exhaust gases were carried upwards through two vertical pipes fitted with non-return valves. Even though the invasion was cancelled the experiments were put to good use by 18th Panzer Division the following year during its amphibious assault crossing of the River Bug.

From 1942 onwards no army paid as much attention to every aspect of armoured assault engineering as did the British. This stemmed in part from the knowledge that when it returned to the continent of Europe it would have to breach the formidable defences of the Atlantic Wall, and in this respect the Dieppe Raid confirmed beyond any reasonable doubt that without specially designed AFVs the task would involve horrific loss of life, if it could be achieved at all. It also stemmed from sheer necessity, for in the Western Desert steadily increasing use of anti-tank mines had actually begun to dictate the nature of the fighting.

Minefields could be gapped by hand, but the process was laborious and, since they were covered by defensive fire, casualties among the sappers and their infantry escort might be extremely heavy. It was, of course, possible to create a cleared lane by focusing artillery fire or aerial bombing, which would explode the mines, although the effect of this was to tear up the ground in the very place that good going was essential for the passage of armour. In the final analysis, therefore, it was decided that mines were best cleared by an AFV with

Right: The Soviet SU-76 self-propelled 76.2mm gun was based on the chassis of the T70 light tank and remained in service for some years after the war. This example was captured by United Nations troops in Korea. (USAMHI)

Right: Schwimmpanzer III, designed for submerged wading, undergoing trials during the preparations for the aborted invasion of the United Kingdom, Operation 'Sea-lion'. (Bundesarchiv)

Left: Grant Scorpion III mineclearing flail tank, a number of which saw service during the closing months of the campaign in Tunisia. (National Army Museum)

equipment specially designed for the task. Several ideas were tested, including heavy rollers pushed ahead of a tank, detonating the mines by their weight; ploughs which turned the mines out of the tank's path; and hoses which were fired across the minefield by rocket, pumped full of liquid explosive and then detonated, the nearest mines being exploded by the seismic shock wave. None of these, however, produced as consistently good results as flailing, in which the ground ahead of the tank was beaten by weighted chains swung from a power-driven rotating drum which was itself attached to the tank's hull. The first operational flail was the Matilda Scorpion, twelve of which were employed during the Second Battle of Alamein, and later in the campaign a number of Grants were similarly converted. The Scorpions were fitted with auxiliary external engines which drove the rotating drum, but this unsatisfactory feature was eliminated with the development in June 1943 of the Sherman Crab whose rotor was driven by a power take-off from the tank's main engine. Within limits, the Scorpions and the Crab retained the ability to use their turret guns when not actually flailing, although since their purpose was obvious and their maximum operational speed only 1.5mph they tended to attract heavy fire unless properly supported. The Crab was capable of detonating mines to a depth of five inches, each mine simultaneously destroying the chain that had struck it.

Detailed study of the Atlantic Wall revealed that when the Allies landed they would face not only extensive minefields but also formidable physical obstacles which included concrete bunker complexes, conventional sea defences supplemented by shaped concrete walls designed to prevent vehicles leaving the beach, backed by anti-tank ditches and roads so deeply cratered as to be unusable. It was decided, therefore, to design a multi-purpose armoured assault engineer vehicle capable, in its various forms, of overcoming all these obstructions. The result was the AVRE (Armoured Vehicle Royal Engineers), based on the hull of the Churchill

Left: The Sherman Crab, shown here working with its turret traversed to the rear, was the most efficient flail tank of the war. (RAC Tank Museum)

Right: AVRE of 79th Armoured Division with its Small Box Girder (SBG) Bridge lowered in harbour area. North-west Europe, winter 1944/5. (IWM)

infantry tank, which was both roomy and possessed a superb cross-country performance. The AVRE's turret mounted a muzzle-loading 290mm Petard Mortar capable of firing a 40lb bomb to a distance of approximately 90 yards; this was normally used to shatter or crack open concrete bunkers or pillboxes. It was, however, the AVRE's standardized external fittings that rendered the vehicle so versatile, as these enabled it to carry a variety of assault engineering devices including a 20ft box girder bridge which could be placed against a sea wall, so forming a ramp for other AFVs; a bobbin

which unrolled flexible track ahead of the vehicle, thus improving the going on soft areas of beach; a fascine which could be dropped into an anti-tank ditch and serve as a causeway across, a method which had served well at Cambrai in 1917; and frames mounting heavy demolition charges which could be placed against a fortification and then detonated by remote control after the vehicle had reversed to a safe distance. A variation on the obstacle-crossing theme was provided by the Ark, a turretless Churchill fitted with folding ramps forward and aft. This was driven bodily into the obstacle, which might be a watercourse or a

Above: Valentine scissors bridgelayer. Although the design was too small for use in Europe, it proved invaluable during the latter stages of the campaign in Burma. (IWM)

Right: An AVRE carrying a fascine on a launching sledge is prepared for action by its crew on the II Polish Corps sector of the Italian front, 1945. (Sikorski Museum)

Right: A troop of M.10 tank destroyers crosses a river on a causeway of Churchill ARKs during the closing stages of the Italian campaign. (IWM)

deep crater in a road, the ramps being unfolded to form a bridge; if the obstacle were particularly deep two Arks might be employed, one on top of the other.

The Churchill also served as the basis for the most terrible flame-thrower of the war, the Crocodile. The basic vehicle was the Churchill Mk VII to which was coupled a two-wheeled armoured trailer containing 400 gallons of fuel and cylinders of nitrogen propellant gas. From the trailer a pipe led under the tank's belly into the driving compartment where it joined the flame-gun. On leaving the flame-gun the fuel was ignited electrically and propelled in a jet up to 120 yards, the blazing liquid clinging tenaciously to everything it touched. No field fortification could hope to survive the combined onslaught of AVREs and Crocodiles; in fact, once the latter's distinctive trailers had been identified, few of the defenders had any inclination to put the matter to the test.

The need for gun tanks to be got ashore as quickly as possible was appreciated by the Allied planners as it had been by the Germans, but the means of achieving this were very different. Submerged wading

Left: Crocodile firing a flame shot during training. The arrival of these terrifying vehicles was often in itself sufficient to induce surrender. (RAC Tank Museum)

was never seriously considered, and external flotation tanks were so bulky that they seriously reduced on-shore mobility. It was decided, therefore, to adopt an ingenious buoyancy system devised by Mr. Nicholas Straussler. This involved fitting the tank with a collapsible canvas screen braced by horizontal rails and locked in position by mechanical struts, the screen being raised by flexible pneumatic hoses which straightened and lifted its upper rail when filled with compressed air. This system provided sufficient freeboard for operation in conditions up to sea state five, beyond which the waves broke over the screen and began to fill its interior. Propulsion afloat was effected by steerable propellers driven off the tank's gearbox, giving a speed of four knots. Once the shallows had been reached the struts were unlocked and the compressed air released, causing the screen to collapse, and the drive was transferred to the tracks, thus enabling the tank to go straight into action with its fighting qualities unimpaired.

Tanks so equipped were designated DD, standing for Duplex Drive, which served as a thin cover for their real purpose.

Right: Valentine DDs with flotation screens erected, showing air pillars and bracing struts. The vehicle was used mainly for training, but by 1944 was clearly under-gunned and was replaced by the Sherman DD. (IWM)

Experiments were carried out with the Stuart and the Valentine, but neither possessed the punch required and some months before D-Day it was decided that the standard DD would be the Sherman. The intention was that the parent LSTs would launch their DDs some way off the invasion beach. The tanks would then swim ashore, almost invisible amid the landing craft, and suppress the fire of the nearest defences from the shallows. This would be followed by the arrival of LSTs which would land their Crab and AVRE assault teams directly on to the beach. In the event, sea conditions on D-Day were atrocious, and although many DDs were launched successfully, some LST commanders considered the risks too great and landed their charges at the waterline; on the American sector conditions were so bad that only half of the DDs launched succeeded in reaching the shore.

In the British Army specialist armoured units were referred to collectively as The Funnies, and in Normandy and north-west Europe were administered by Major-General Sir Percy Hobart's 79th Armoured Division. Before transferring to the then Royal Tank Corps, Hobart had served with the Bengal Sappers and Miners and was thus unusually well qualified for his task; indeed, while his division was training, he was personally involved in the development of much of its equipment and evolved many of its successful battle drills. On active service the division functioned rather like a plant hire corporation, assessing the assault engineering requirements of British, Canadian and, occasionally, American formations, and then supplying specialist teams for the duration of the operation. In Italy 25 Armoured Engineer Brigade, formed in January 1945, performed the same function for the British Eighth Army.

The American Army was less interested in armoured assault engineering vehicles, although it made some use of DD tanks and produced many interesting prototypes. In the Pacific war zone, however, the US Marine Corps developed a family of amphibious AFVs to meet the specific needs of its island-hopping campaign. The

essence of the problem was that many of the Japanese-held islands were girdled by coral reefs which prevented conventional landing craft from reaching the shore proper. Even if the craft could be grounded on the reef, and the lagoon between it and the shoreline was suitably shallow, the invasion force would still have to wade a considerable distance in the teeth of the enemy's fire. Fortunately, foresight had provided the means of overcoming these difficulties, as the Corps had already recognized the potential of a tracked amphibious swamp rescue vehicle designed by a Florida engineer, Mr. Donald Roebling. The military versions of the design were designated LVTs (Landing Vehicles Tracked) or Amtracs (Amphibious Tractors) and were first used operationally as unarmoured ship-to-shore stores ferries during the Guadalcanal campaign. It was soon appreciated that an armoured version could cross reefs, wade lagoons and land riflemen above the tide line in comparative safety. Likewise, additional versions armed with heavy fire support weapons could play a decisive part in suppressing local strongpoints, but could also accompany the advance inland until tanks could be landed. The Japanese were always ready to fight to the death, but they were unprepared for the LVT, the use of which saved thousands of American lives at Tarawa, Kwajalein, Saipan, Tinian, Guam, Peleliu and Iwo Jima.

Large numbers of LVTs were also supplied to the British Army, which referred to them as Buffaloes in north-west Europe and as Fantails in Italy. At its greatest strength the 79th Armoured Division could dispose of no less than five LVT regiments. The most important LVT operations in north-west Europe included assault landings on South Beveland and Walcheren during the clearance of the Scheldt estuary; Operation 'Veritable', the clearance of the Reichswald forest and the left bank of the Rhine; and Operation 'Plunder', 21st Army Group's crossing of the Rhine. In Italy the Eighth Army formed a provisional LVT regiment from surplus tank drivers and transport personnel and in April 1945 this carried out an assault

Right: Sherman DD of the US 753rd Tank Battalion with flotation screen lowered, Italy 1944. On 15 August 1944 the battalion took part in the Allied landings on the Mediterranean coast of France. (USAMHI)

Right: LVTs played a critical part in amphibious operations in the Pacific theatre of war and, as shown here, were also employed in north-west Europe by 79th Armoured Division. (RAC Tank Museum)

landing across Lake Comacchio during the final offensive of the campaign.

THE TANK'S ENEMIES

It goes almost without saying that the tank's most implacable enemy was its own kind, yet many other equally obvious weapon systems were ranged against it, including anti-tank guns, medium artillery, purpose-built tank destroyers, up-gunned assault guns, mines, close-quarter infantry weapons and ground-attack aircraft.

Anti-tank gunners began the war armed with weapons ranging in calibre from 25mm to 50mm, a majority of armies opting for 37mm guns. These weapons had been designed during the 1930s, when the tank's armour was still comparatively thin, and, since much emphasis had rightly been placed on their rapid emplacement and concealment, they were small, light and easily handled by their crews. However, as the effects of the gun/armour spiral began to bite and the tank's armour became progressively thicker, larger guns were

required to penetrate it and the calibre of weapons rose through 75mm to 100mm and, in one instance, to 128mm. In theory, the process of fitting more powerful guns to larger and larger carriages had no limits, although in practice it was governed by the gun crew's ability to handle their weapon; the British towed 17pdr anti-tank gun, for example, required many hours of hard work before it was properly emplaced and dug in. The use of muzzle brakes enabled carriage weights to be kept to a minimum, but despite this by 1944 the average weight of anti-tank guns had risen to somewhere between two and three tons, while the size of the weapons themselves had trebled since 1939. This represented the outer limits of what was practicable. In passing, it is worth mentioning that two of the best tank-killers of the war had not begun their service lives as anti-tank guns at all. The famed German Eighty-Eight (88mm) had been designed as a towed anti-aircraft gun and its first engagements in the anti-tank role had been undertaken out of dire necessity. It possessed excellent sights and was capable of penetrating any tank in service at a range that its opponents could not match until the issue of HE tank ammunition became general during the

Below: Fitted with excellent sights for use in the ground role, the German 88mm anti-aircraft gun was one of the finest tank killers of the war. Its major disadvantages were the difficulty involved in towing it across broken or soft going, and the fact that it was high-standing and vulnerable. (RAC Tank Museum)

second half of the war. The Eighty-Eight's principal disadvantages were its lack of mobility over poor going, and the fact that it was high-standing and vulnerable. The British 25pdr gun/howitzer was, of course, a field artillery weapon which, in the Western Desert, carried a number of AP rounds in its limber for self-defence. During direct engagements between 25pdr regiments and the Africa Corps' panzer divisions the former obtained spectacularly successful results on a number of occasions, notably on 25 November 1941, when 1st Field Regiment RA beat off several determined attacks by 5th Panzer Regiment.

Anti-tank guns were most effective when combined with other arms in both attack and defence. The Germans preferred to use them aggressively and deployed them well forward near their tanks, forming what they called PaK Fronts (PaK = Panzer abwehr Kanone, or anti-tank gun) on to which the enemy armour could be lured by a withdrawal, feigned or otherwise. For many years the British believed that they had been out-gunned during the tank battles in the Western Desert, but the truth was that much of the damage was being caused by distant Eighty-Eights or nearly invisible 75mm PaK 40s. When, on 6 March 1943, Rommel counter-attacked the Eighth Army at Medenine with 10th, 15th and 21st Panzer Divisions, he discovered that his enemies had learned their lesson well. In the words of the British official history: 'The anti-tank guns had at last been sited to kill tanks and not to "protect" infantry, field guns, or anything else. Some 3.7in AA guns had been added to the anti-tank guns, and no 25pdrs had been saddled with an anti-tank task.' There were also 350 field and medium artillery weapons available, and several armoured brigades were on call close behind the front. The Axis attack made no progress at all and at 2030 hours Rommel gave the order to retire. Medenine was the last battle he fought in Africa and it cost him a minimum of 44 tanks for no return.

From Second Alamein onwards, the capacity of the British and American armies to switch heavy artillery concentrations around the battlefield also proved a potent factor in the anti-tank defence. In Tunisia it was discovered that not even the crews of the mighty Tiger E, immune to most anti-tank weapons, were prepared to put up with a hammering from 5.5in howitzer shells for very long. During the subsequent

Below: 3rd County of London Yeomanry crews examine a captured PaK 40 75mm anti-tank gun. Much of the gun's camouflage has been blown away, but enough remains to show how well it was concealed to blend in with its background. Italy, 1943. (National Army Museum)

campaigns in Sicily, Italy and Western Europe it became customary to respond to the presence of Tigers with medium artillery concentrations or, where appropriate, naval gunfire and air strikes.

From 1939 until 1941 the Army of still-neutral United States had studied the German *Blitzkrieg* technique at the highest levels and had correctly concluded that once defensive fronts had been broken the panzer divisions moved too quickly for fresh fronts to be established across their path with towed anti-tank guns. The tank itself offered one solution to the problem, but the Chief of the Armored Force was training his troops specifically for offensive operations and did not wish to see his vehicles deployed in a defensive role. On the other hand, the anti-tank gun was potentially a more powerful weapon than that carried by the majority of contemporary tanks, and if it could be given a self-propelled mobility it could be deployed and re-deployed to deal with any developing crisis, which the towed gun could not. This was accepted by the Army's Chief of Staff, General George C. Marshall, who also recognized that solving the problem lay 'beyond the capabilities of any one arm and probably required the organization and use

Below: British 2pdr crew training in the Western Desert. By 1941 the gun was rapidly becoming obsolete, but anti-tank gunners were forced to soldier on with it until the 6pdr began reaching the front the following year. (IWM)

Right: British 2pdr *portée* in the Western Desert. Although never intended to fight as tank destroyers, portée-equipped units often found themselves performing the role in their unprotected vehicles.

of a special force of combined arms, capable of rapid movement, interception and active rather than passive defense tactics'.

The Tank Destroyer Force was established in 1941 under Lieutenant Colonel (later Major General) Andrew D. Bruce, who was, in effect, required to form a new arm of service, formulate its doctrine, organize its training, superintend its weapons development and prepare its tables of organization. From the outset the basic thinking behind the new arm was simple. Large numbers of tank destroyers were to be deployed rapidly in the path and on the flanks of any penetration by enemy armour, where they would destroy their opponents by direct gunfire. The basic unit was the battalion, which consisted of a headquarters company, three gun companies and a reconnaissance company; higher formations included the Tank Destroyer Group, consisting of a Group Headquarters and three TD battalions, and the Tank Destroyer Brigade, which included a Headquarters and two Tank Destroyer Groups.

Bruce was also clear about the sort of weapon system he was looking for. 'What we are after is a fast-moving vehicle, armed with a weapon with a powerful punch which can be easily and quickly fired, and in the last analysis we would like to get armored protection against small-arms fire so that this weapon cannot be put out of action by a machine-gun.' At first, however, the TDF had to put up with expedient weapons. The 37mm Gun Motor Carriage M6 was a light tank destroyer based on a 15cwt truck and was very similar in layout to the British 2pdr *portées* already fighting in the Western Desert; some of these vehicles served in North Africa, although the light class of tank destroyer was phased out as heavier weapons became available. The 75mm Gun Motor Carriage M3 con-sisted of the elderly French M1897–A4 75mm gun, of which the US Army retained a stock of several hundred, fitted to the M3 halftrack APC on a limited traverse mounting. This vehicle also served in North Africa until replaced by the 3in Gun Motor Carriage M10, which employed the chassis of the M4A2 medium tank series. The M10 was built to the Tank Destroyer Board's specification and had an angled hull and an open-topped turret capable of all-round traverse. It remained the best-known Allied tank destroyer of the war, more than 6,700 being built, and was also supplied to the British, French and Soviet Armies.

Nevertheless, the appearance of the Tiger meant that the TDF required an even more powerful weapon. A 90mm high-velocity anti-aircraft gun was chosen for the task, but the standard M10 turret could not house this, so a new turret was designed and fitted to the M10 chassis, the vehicle being accepted as standard and designated the 90mm Gun Motor Carriage M36 in June 1944. The vehicle which came closest to Bruce's ideal tank destroyer, however, was the 19-ton 76mm Gun Motor Carriage M18, which had been purpose-built from the ground up. The M18 employed a torsion bar suspension and was driven by a 400hp Continental engine which produced a road

Above: When the M3 had been replaced by purpose-built tank destroyers in the US Army, a number were taken into British service and issued to armoured car regiments, where they served in Heavy Troops. In Italy these often found themselves serving as supplementary artillery. (USAMHI)

Left: An historic photograph showing part of the US 601st Tank Destroyer Battalion at El Guettar, Tunisia, shortly before it defeated a counter-attack by 10th Panzer Division on 23 March 1943. During the engagement the 601st destroyed 38 tanks at the cost of 21 of its 31 M3 75mm tank destroyers. Note the excellent hull-down position taken up by the M3 in the background. (USAMHI)

Right: The Gun Motor Carriage M10, here shown with its 3in gun locked in the rear travelling clamp, became the best known of all American tank destroyers. The weapon bore down heavily on the forward edge of the turret and to restore balance the latter was fitted with counter-weights on its rear face. (IWM)

Above: The Gun Motor Carriage was armed with a 90mm gun which required a larger turret with a pronounced overhang. At 1,000 yards the gun could penetrate six inches of armour; at the same range, using two rounds, it could penetrate five feet of reinforced concrete. (RAC Tank Museum)

Below: An M10 troop firing in the supplementary artillery role during the Italian campaign. The static nature of the fighting is emphasized by the bivouac and the quantity of expended ammunition cases. (USAMHI)

Right: The Gun Motor Carriage M18 (Hellcat), armed with a 76mm gun, was the fastest tracked AFV of its day and came closest to the TDF's concept of the ideal tank destroyer. (RAC Tank Museum)

speed of 60mph, making it the fastest tracked AFV of the war and earning it the unofficial name of Hellcat. It was armed with the same 76mm gun that was being developed for the later models of the M4 Sherman medium tank, housed in an open-topped turret. The M18 began entering service in the autumn of 1943 and was highly regarded by its crews both for its performance in action and its built-in ease of maintenance.

Unfortunately, by the time the TDF took the field the day of the German mass tank attack was over. Despite this, there were sufficient incidents in which TD battalions halted local counter-attacks by German armour to see that the concept would have worked, had the need arisen. Tank destroyer battalions fought in North Africa, Italy, Europe and the Pacific. When not engaged in the anti-tank role their tasks included long-range direct shooting, bunker-busting, providing supplementary artillery fire and supporting infantry attacks.

The British Army's 2pdr *portées* were not

designed as tank destroyers but rather as a means of eliminating the damage which would have been caused as a result of towing the weapon across rough desert going by mounting the gun on the back of a truck. Although it was not the intention that the guns should be fought mounted it was often more convenient to do so, although the risks involved sometimes verged on the suicidal. The 6pdr anti-tank gun could also be carried *portée* and an armoured version of this, known as the Deacon, was issued on the scale of one battery per anti-tank

regiment, its official role being that of mobile anti-tank reserve. By June 1943 the Deacons were obsolete and were being replaced steadily by the American M10, which was known as the Wolverine in British service. Meanwhile, work was continuing on the first British tracked tank destroyer to enter service, the Archer. This consisted of the excellent British 17pdr anti-tank gun fitted to the chassis of the obsolete Valentine infantry tank so as to fire over the vehicle's tail, an inconvenient arrangement which involved reversing into its firing position. As the numbers of Archers serving with units began to rise after October 1944 many M10s were withdrawn so that their 3in guns could be replaced with the more powerful 17pdr, the composite vehicle being known as the Achilles.

During the last years of the war the British used their tank destroyers for the same tasks as the Americans, but did not form special units with them. Instead, the composition of corps and divisional anti-tank regiments incorporated both towed anti-tank guns (6pdr or 17pdr) and tank destroyers (M10 or Achilles). Because of the difficulties involved in emplacing the towed 17pdr it was decided to employ M10s to form anti-tank gun screens both during the Normandy landings and the subsequent fighting in the close bocage country. Likewise, in Italy, Normandy and north-west Europe, the tank destroyer

Below: The Archer tank destroyer was based on the Valentine tank chassis and was armed with the excellent 17pdr gun. The principal disadvantage of the vehicle was its limited-traverse mounting, which meant that it had to be reversed into its firing position. (RAC Tank Museum)

provided a means of getting anti-tank weapons forward quickly while the infantry consolidated a captured objective.

The German Army paid little attention to tank destroyer development until forced to do so by its encounters with the heavily armoured British Matilda and, more important, with the Soviet T-34/76 medium and KV heavy tanks, both of which were impervious to and outranged the German tank guns then in service. It would take time before larger tank guns could be fitted to redress the balance, and the gap could not be filled by towed anti-tank weapons since these either lacked the mobility to keep pace with the armoured element of the panzer divisions or were not powerful enough for what was required of them. There was, therefore, a sudden and desperate need for fully mobile anti-tank guns to penetrate these formidable opponents. Luckily, quantity production of

Above: The Marder I consisted of a marriage between the chassis of the French Lorraine tracked carrier and the German PaK 40/1 75mm anti-tank gun. (Bundesarchiv)

Left: The Marder III tank destroyer employed the chassis of the obsolete Pz Kpfw 38(t) and was armed with a captured Russian Model 36 76.2mm gun rechambered to take German 75mm ammunition. (US National Archives)

Above: Largest of the first generation of German tank destroyers was the Nashorn (rhinoceros), based on the Pz Kpfw IV chassis and armed with an 88mm PaK 43/1 gun. This example was captured by Canadian troops on the Pontecorvo sector of the Hitler Line, 26 May 1944; unfortunately, the censor has eliminated every item of information that would permit identification of the unit involved. (Public Archives of Canada)

75mm anti-tank guns was well under way and a stock of captured Russian weapons was also available. Equally fortunate was the fact that a substantial number of obsolete German, Czech and French tank chassis were to hand, and the logical solution was to combine the two.

The first generation of German tank destroyers all followed the same pattern, consisting of a gun fitted to a tank chassis on a limited traverse mounting, with the fighting compartment protected by a fixed open-topped superstructure of armour plate. Most of these conversions, despite their varied origins and appearance, were named Marder (marten). Marder I was based on a French chassis and was armed with the 75mm PaK 40/1. Marder II was based either on the chassis of the Pz Kpfw II Models A, B, C, F, in which case it was armed with the 75mm PaK 40/2, or that of the Pz Kpfw II Models D and E, which mounted a Russian Model 36 76.2mm gun re-chambered to take the German 75mm

round. The Marder III employed the chassis of the Pz Kpfw 38(t); early models were also armed with the Russian gun, but later in the series this was replaced by the German 75mm PaK 40/3, which had a similar performance. The largest of the interim tank destroyer designs was the Nashorn (rhinoceros), which mounted the 88mm PaK 43/1 on a front-engined Pz Kpfw IV chassis incorporating the transmission and final drive of the Pz Kpfw III. This extremely powerful weapon system was issued to 30-strong heavy tank destroyer battalions which were at the disposal of army commanders.

Even as these stop-gap vehicles entered service in 1942–3, work was proceding on a second generation of tank destroyers. Unlike their American counterparts, German designers were prepared to trade off the advantages of a turret with all-round traverse for the ability to mount a more powerful weapon in a fixed, fully enclosed fighting compartment, which conferred the additional benefits of simplified construction and reduced height. The first of the new tank destroyers, the Jagdpanzer IV, was based on the Pz Kpfw IV chassis and armed first with the 75mm PaK 39 and then with the longer 75mm KwK 42. It began entering service towards the end of 1943 and gradually replaced the Marders in the tank destroyer battalions of the panzer divisions. The Hetzer (troublemaker), which employed the Pz Kpfw 38(t) chassis and was armed with the 75mm PaK 39, began entering service with the tank destroyer battalions of the infantry divisions in 1944. The replacement for the Nashorn in the heavy tank destroyer battalions, the Jagdpanther, also began reaching the front in 1944; this was based on the Panther tank chassis and was armed with an 88mm PaK 43/3 mounted in a well-angled superstructure.

Even more powerful was the Jagdtiger, which employed the Tiger B chassis, was armed with a 128mm PaK 80 and weighed more than 70 tons; this vehicle suffered chronic transmission problems and very few were built. Somewhat apart from the mainstream of tank destroyer development was the Elefant, also known as Ferdinand, which was actually the failed Porsche candidate for the Tiger tank series, and was armed with an 88mm PaK 43/2 mounted in a heavily armoured superstructure aft. The Elefant had a disastrous debut during the great tank battle at Kursk in July 1943, when two battalions were employed in the breakthrough role. Lacking machine-guns for local defence, many fell victim to Soviet tank-hunting teams armed with flame-throwers, Molotov cocktails and explosive devices. The survivors were sent to the Italian front, where their size, 67-ton

Right: The Hetzer was armed with the 75mm PaK 39. The vehicle possessed an excellent ballistic profile, but off-setting the gun so far to the right imposed operating difficulties on the crew, since the weapon had itself been designed for loading from the right. The Hetzer served with the tank destroyer battalions of infantry divisions, in this case an SS division. (Bundesarchiv)

Right: The Jagdpanther (left) also possessed good ballistic lines and provides an interesting contrast in tank destroyer design with the American GMC M36 (right).

Right: The Elefant, armed with an 88mm PaK 43/2, fared badly during its operational début at Kursk in July 1943. Survivors such as this were modified by the addition of a machine-gun for local defence and sent to the Italian front. (Bundesarchiv)

Left: The Jagdpanzer IV was the first of the second generation of German tank destroyers and, as its name suggests, also employed the Pz Kpfw IV chassis. Early models, such as this, were armed with the 75mm PaK 39, but this was subsequently replaced by the more powerful 75mm KwK 42. Note the coating of *Zimmerit* anti-magnetic paste. (RAC Tank Museum)

weight and low speed of 12mph were less of a disadvantage in the semi-static conditions of mountain warfare.

The German tank destroyer battalion consisted of a headquarters battery and three gun batteries, each containing three three-gun troops. Tank destroyer units serving with the infantry remained on a captured objective until it had been consolidated against counter-attack and then moved back into reserve. If the infantry were attacked, the tank destroyers would be committed where the danger from the enemy armour was greatest, adding their fire to that of the emplaced anti-tank guns. During a withdrawal, their mobility made them an essential part of the rearguard, enabling them to retire through a succession of tactical bounds into the new front line. When working with the panzer divisions the tank destroyers would form a firm base during the advance, as well as covering its flanks. If the tanks were successful, the tank destroyers would move forward and establish a new gun line from which to support the next phase. In the event of an enemy penetration, the tank destroyers might either delay the enemy armour at a holding line while friendly tanks mounted a flank attack, or operate against its flanks themselves.

From its inception the Panzerwaffe had been opposed to providing tank support for infantry operations. The infantry, however, were entitled to expect armoured support, and indeed could not function properly without it, and to remedy this defect the specialist Sturmartillerie (assault artillery) was formed. This branch of service was equipped with specially designed, low-slung assault guns (*Sturmgeschütz*, generally shortened to StuG) based on the chassis of the Pz Kpfw III and armed with a short 75mm howitzer housed in an enclosed superstructure mounted well forward. These took the field first in battery strength then, as more became available, in battalions and finally brigades. They played no part in the Polish campaign of 1939, but four batteries took part in the 1940 campaign in the west, three battalions fought in the 1941 Balkan campaigns, and six battalions participated in Operation

Above: One of the four Sturmartillerie batteries which took part in the 1940 campaign in western Europe. (RAC Tank Museum)

Below: Experience on the Eastern Front led to the StuG's short howitzer being replaced by a 75mm L/43 then a 75mm L/48 gun with armour-defeating capabilities. This meant that while the StuG retained its infantry support role it simultaneously became an extremely efficient tank destroyer. (RAC Tank Museum)

Right: The StuG's low profile made it a very dangerous opponent, since it could easily be concealed in folds of the ground or even among standing crops. This example was knocked out in Italy. (Public Archives of Canada)

Left: Latterly the Italian Army made greater use of its assault guns than it did of its obsolete tanks. This example is the Semovente 75/18, based on the M13/40 medium tank chassis and armed with a 75mm gun. (RAC Tank Museum)

Left: The Semovente M43, armed with a 105mm howitzer, was based on the chassis of the M14/41 medium tank. After the Italian surrender many were employed by German panzergrenadier formations serving in Italy. (RAC Tank Museum)

Left: The Soviet Army's SU-100 tank destroyer, based on the T-34 chassis and armed with a 100mm gun.

Left: The ISU-122 tank destroyer employed the IS heavy tank chassis and was armed with a 122mm gun. (IWM)

'Barbarossa'. Thereafter the numbers rose steadily.

The impact of the T-34/76 and the KV was as severely felt by the Sturmartillerie as it had been by the panzer divisions, since its short howitzers were quite incapable of defeating the Russian armour. On the other hand it was able to react more quickly to the threat because the assault gun's roomy interior enabled it to be re–fitted with longer 75mm guns which were capable of penetrating the enemy vehicles. This gave the assault gun a dual role as a tank destroyer, although its original purpose remained, and in 1943 a small proportion were equipped with a 105mm howitzer. By the spring of 1944 it was estimated that the Sturmartillerie had destroyed some 20,000 enemy tanks, the majority on the Eastern Front. In Italy and the west the distinction between German assault guns and purpose-built tank destroyers became so blurred in Allied eyes that both were simply reported as SPs. During the final stages of the war the tank shortage was such that in some cases one of the panzer regiment's two battalions was equipped with assault guns.

The Soviet Army was quick to see the advantages inherent in the assault gun's layout and built several assault gun/tank destroyers to the same pattern. Of these the most important were the SU-85 and SU-100 based on the T-34 chassis, armed respectively with 85mm and 100mm high-velocity guns, the ISU-122 tank destroyer, based on the IS heavy tank chassis and armed with a 122mm gun, and the ISU-152 assault howitzer, which also employed the IS chassis and was known as The Animal Killer because of the number of Tigers and Elefants it destroyed at Kursk. Units equipped with these vehicles were either integrated into a defence in depth or employed in the fire support role during set-piece assaults, with particular emphasis on picking off the enemy's tanks at long range.

Mines seldom destroyed a tank completely, but they could cripple it with serious track and suspension damage and render it a sitting target. Naturally, no commander would willingly send his tanks into an uncleared minefield, but mistakes could happen. During the First Battle of Alamein, for example, two regiments of 23 Armoured Brigade were detailed to mount a counter-attack through minefield gaps cleared the previous night. Due to operational difficulties the gaps were not completed and a signal was dispatched to the brigade ordering it to shift the axis of its attack further south across ground which was (mistakenly, as it happened) believed to be clear. The signal was not received and the attack went in along the original axis, with the result that twenty tanks were immediately lost in the minefield. The brigade then came under heavy fire from a PaK Front on Ruweisat Ridge, to its right. German tanks arrived to join in the battle and the survivors were forced to withdraw, losing more vehicles as they re-crossed the minefield. By the end of the day the two regiments' combined loss amounted to 90 Valentines, three Matildas and 44 per cent of their personnel. Yet the density of these minefields was but a fraction of that which confronted the Eighth Army at the start of the Second Battle of Alamein. On 21 October, two days before the battle began, the senior German engineer officer estimated that his men had laid 445,000 mines, of which only 14,000 were of the anti-personnel type. Nor was there any way of avoiding the problem, since the front was locked solid from the sea to the Qattara Depression.

Mines were best used in conjunction with terrain features to channel the advance of the enemy armour. Features such as marshland, defiles, woods, steep hills and badly broken ground would be avoided by tanks as a matter of course, and minefields could be laid in the intervening areas so that the only open and obvious route led on to a killing ground covered by anti-tank guns, artillery and friendly armour. Likewise, mines could be used to impose delay, particularly in mountainous terrain where roads were few and narrow; in these circumstances the removal of a mined tank that was blocking the route could take hours, especially if it was kept under fire.

On the Eastern Front the spaces were vast and the situation too fluid for extensive use to be made of mine warfare. There were exceptions to this, the most notable of which was the Soviet Army's defence in depth of the Kursk Salient, where it laid 2,200 anti-tank and 2,500 anti-personnel mines per mile of front. As a general rule applicable to all theatres of war, however, tanks were at greatest risk from mines in periods of static or semi-static warfare; once the front became mobile engineers had neither the time nor the opportunity to lay minefields of a critical depth or density.

In towns, villages, woodland, scrub and high-standing crops tanks were in danger from the opposing infantry's close-range anti-tank weapons and rarely operated in these areas without the close support of their own organic infantry. Sometimes the infantry had little to offer save bluff, but against inexperienced crews even this could work. In one incident during the Spanish Civil War retreating Republican troops slung a rope across a street and hung blankets on it, blocking the view beyond. Two Italian tankettes, which had hitherto been pressing the Republicans hard, were brought up sharp by their fear of the unknown and opened fire on the blankets. They were joined by a medium tank which opened up with its main armament. After half an hour's heavy firing the rope was cut and the riddled bedclothes fell in a heap, but by then there was not a Republican in sight. A variation on the same theme was the placing of up-turned soup plates across a road, which induced an uneasy feeling in some crews that the enemy had invented a deadly ceramic anti-tank mine.

It did not take infantry very long to discover two important facts about the tank. First, the ground closest to the vehicle, and especially to its immediate rear, could not be covered by its weapons. Secondly, the crew's vision was similarly curtailed over roughly the same area. It followed, therefore, that close-quarter attacks delivered from the rear stood the greatest chance of success, provided the attacker were suitably armed. There are numerous accounts of extremely courageous men who have destroyed a tank by firing into or dropping grenades down an open turret hatch, or placing satchel charges under the turret overhang, or smashing Molotov cocktails against the air intakes; rather more numerous, though unrecorded, are the number of incidents in which the attacker was shot dead by another tank or the escorting infantry before he could do any damage.

It was the Japanese who developed the personal close-quarter attack to its greatest extent, largely because they had little to offer beyond supreme bravery and self-sacrifice. Among the devices they employed were pole charges which they sought to explode against the commander's cupola; hand-placed demolition charges which would blast their way through the engine deck; and frangible glass grenades containing liquid hydrogen cyanide which they hoped would be drawn into the vehicle in vapour form, incapacitating the crew – this last was unsuitable for employment in tropical climates as the fumes dispersed too quickly, and its use in the anti-tank role was not reported after 1942. There were instances, too, of Japanese officers attempting to fight their way into turrets with their swords and, in one case, succeeding. In early 1945 the situation of the Japanese Burma Area Army was so critical that it decided to form what it called Human Tank Destruction Squads, the anti-tank equivalent of the *Kamikaze* pilots. The members of these would either attempt to throw themselves under a tank and blow in its thin belly plates with the charge they carried; or they would sit in a loosely camouflaged hole in a track, a 100lb aerial bomb between their knees, waiting to strike the exposed detonator with a stone the minute a tank passed overhead. These methods had their successes but, thanks to the vigilance of the tank crews and their close infantry escort, they were few and far between.

In Europe, the problem of providing the infantry with close-quarter defence against tanks had been given some thought during the 1930s with the result that most armies began the war armed with anti-tank rifles. These were simply miniature anti-tank guns fired from a bipod. They were heavy to carry, awkward to handle and kicked viciously when fired. On average, they could penetrate 15mm armour at 300 yards, and even by 1939 this was clearly inadequate. The British 0.55in Boys anti-tank rifle claimed a number of Italian tankettes and thinly-armoured Japanese light tanks, but against anything more robust it made no impression.

The real breakthrough in close-quarter anti-tank tactics came with the introduction of hollow- or shaped-charge ammunition from the end of 1942 onwards. This took advantage of the phenomenon known as the Monro Effect, which demonstrated that a conical hole in the end of a cylindrical charge served to focus the explosion of the latter into a narrow jet of immense power which would blast its way through the thickest armour and kill the tank crew; even more power could be obtained if the cone itself were lined with copper. The salient fact about hollow-charge ammunition, which relied on chemical rather than kinetic energy to achieve its effect, was that it did not require a complex and powerful weapon system for its delivery and was therefore suitable for issue to the infantry. The British Army developed a spring-loaded spigot mortar known as the PIAT (Projector Infantry Anti-Tank) from which to launch its shaped-charge bombs, but the Americans produced the much superior Bazooka in which the bomb itself was fitted with a small rocket motor and fired through a tube aimed from the shoulder. The Bazooka was copied by the German Army and given the official title of *Racketenpanzerbuchse*, although it was also referred to as the *Panzerschrek* or *Panzerfaust*. Some defence against shaped-charge rounds could be obtained by fitting side plates and turret girdles which dissipated much of the blast before it reached the main armour, but the practice was not universal and, in general, the effect of these weapons was to place the tank at the mercy of any infantryman so armed within a range of 100 yards, and since tank hunters invariably concealed their presence until the last possible moment the tank was forced to rely on the protection of its own infantry to an even greater extent.

Below: Men of the RAF Regiment training with a PIAT. Weapons such as these, and the much superior Bazooka and *Racketenpanzerbuchse*, provided the infantry with a close-quarter defence against tanks. (RAC Tank Museum)

Finally, as the war continued tanks became more and more at risk from specialist tank-busting wings of tactical ground-support aircraft. These employed a variety of weapons, but cannon were favoured since they were accurate and able to penetrate thinly armoured engine decks and turret roofs with ease. In western Europe the RAF employed rocket-firing Typhoons; the rockets themselves were inaccurate and thus unsuitable for use against individual tanks, but each exploded with the force of a medium artillery shell and their use played havoc with the German supply echelons, without which the panzer divisions were unable to function properly. The Luftwaffe probably destroyed more AFVs than any other air force, one ace being credited with the destruction of 519 Soviet tanks, but as the air offensive against Germany gathered weight it was steadily withdrawn from the various fronts for the defence of the homeland leaving the Allied and Soviet air forces to control the skies. The German Army fitted several tank and halftrack chassis with anti-aircraft mountings, but these could not alter the fact of Allied air supremacy.

From 1939 until 1942 the tank had dominated the world's battlefields, but by 1943 so many enemies were ranged against it that the nature of the battles it was required to fight was radically different from that of the early years. Prior to 1943, the majority of tank kills were made with armour-piercing shot. Subsequently, while this type of ammunition remained the most important tank killer, whether fired from tanks, tank destroyers or anti-tank guns, it accounted for only 40 per cent of losses. Next came shaped-charge ammunition with 25 per cent, then mines with 16 per cent, followed by medium artillery, air attack and abandonment through various causes, in approximately equal proportions. During the latter half of the war the tank remained the supremely important weapon of land warfare, although it fought as a member of an interdependent team each member of which was responsible for solving some of the others' problems.

Below: The Hawker Typhoon, armed with cannon, rockets and bombs, was the scourge of German armoured formations during the campaign in Normandy. (IWM)

2. Outstanding Designs

PANZERKAMPF-WAGEN IV

Weight: 25 tons
Speed: 26mph
Armour: 80mm
Armament: one 75mm L/48 gun; two
    7.92 machine-guns
Engine: Maybach HL120 TRM 300hp
    petrol
Crew: 5.
(Specification for Model H)

The Pz Kpfw IV has the distinction of being the only tank design to serve throughout the Second World War and for many years after. In 1934 the German Army issued its specification for a close support tank armed with a 75mm L/24 howitzer with which to equip the heavy companies of the panzer battalions, the idea being that the vehicle would eliminate anti-tank guns delaying the advance of the medium tank companies, which at this period were unable to fire high-explosive ammunition. The contract was awarded to the Krupp organization, which incorporated a number of features from its unsuccessful design for the Pz Kpfw III, including the hull, turret and suspension; as finalized after discussion, the last consisted of eight small diameter road wheels suspended in pairs from leaf-spring units. Production commenced in 1936 but comparatively few had been built by the time war broke out.

Below: The Pz Kpfw IV was the only tank design to serve throughout the war. In its original form it was intended to perform the close support role and, armed with a 75mm L/24 howitzer, equipped the heavy companies of panzer battalions. (RAC Tank Museum)

The Model A was protected by 14.5mm armour, increased to 30mm on Models B, C and D, but active service in Poland quickly revealed that this was inadequate and the Model E saw the addition of 30mm *appliqué* plate.

The Model F, introduced in 1941, had 50mm integral armour, supplemented by 30mm *appliqué* plate in the Model G of 1942, standardized as 80mm integral armour with the introduction of the Model H the following year. In the meantime, encounters with the British Matilda and the Soviet T-34/76 and KV Series had led to urgent demands for up-gunning and since the vehicle's turret ring was wide enough to accommodate a high-velocity gun of the same calibre as the short howitzer it was decided that the Pz Kpfw IV would gradually assume the role of main battle tank from the Pz Kpfw III, pending the arrival of the Panther. The 75mm L/43 gun was therefore fitted to the Model F, vehicles

so armed being designated Model F2; at first the L/43 was fitted with a simple single-baffle muzzle brake, but this was replaced by a more efficient double-baffle system. Further up-gunning took place as the improved 75mm L/48 gun became available, this being fitted to later Model Gs and subsequent versions as well as older models when they were returned to Germany for refit. In its final form the Pz Kpfw IV was fitted with side skirts and a turret girdle as a defence against shaped-charge ammunition. The combined effect of up-gunning and up-armouring was an increase in weight which reduced mobility and overloaded the leaf-spring suspension to the point at which the tank tended to yaw even when no steering was applied.

The Pz Kpfw IV design incorporated a number of interesting points. The turret was offset slightly to the left of the vehicle's centre-line, so permitting the drive shaft connecting the engine with the gearbox to

Above: Rear view of captured Pz Kpfw IV Model H. (RAC Tank Museum)

Above: Upper view of Pz Kpfw IV Model H fitted with a full set of side skirts and turret girdle as a defence against shaped-charge ammunition. (RAC Tank Museum)

clear the rotary base junction, through which power was supplied to the turret's electrical systems. An electrical power traverse was fitted, and to keep the vehicle's batteries fully charged without recourse to the main engine a two-stroke auxiliary generator was housed in the engine compartment. An electrical self-starter was provided, but if this failed or severe cold had stiffened the resistance of the sump oil there was also an inertia starter, the handle of which entered the engine compartment through the stern plate; the handle was swung by two men until the flywheel had reached 60rpm, when the power was tripped to turn the main engine. The longer 75mm guns lay muzzle-heavy in their mounting, and to compensate this a compression spring in a cylinder was mounted on the right/forward quadrant of the turret ring and connected to the gun. In some respects the Pz Kpfw IV's gunnery equipment was very sophisticated

for its day. Turret position indicators, driven from the turret rack and employing the counter-rotation principle, were available to both the commander and gunner, enabling target positions to be noted in advance and engaged in rapid succession; howitzer-armed models were also equipped with a clinometer. Further interesting features included a gun position indicator which warned the driver whenever the weapon was traversed over the side, and a rack of smoke-bombs mounted on the stern plate, released by pull-wires as the situation demanded.

More than 8,000 Pz Kpfw IVs were built from 1939 to 1944. During the latter half of the war they equipped one of the panzer regiment's two battalions, and the Panther the other; as the overall situation deteriorated it sometimes became necessary to combine both types of gun tanks in one battalion and equip the second with assault guns. A submerged wading

Above: In some armies the Pz Kpfw IV continued to serve long after the Second World War. This Syrian vehicle was captured on the Golan Heights in June 1967. (Eshel Dramit Ltd)

version was produced for the aborted invasion of the United Kingdom and later used in Russia. Other derivatives included command, artillery observation and armoured recovery vehicles. The chassis also served as the basis for a wide variety of conversions, including assault guns, tank destroyers, the Hummel 150mm self-propelled howitzer, several anti-aircraft vehicles and a series of experimental weapons carriers.

The Pz Kpfw IV remained active with the Finnish and Spanish Armies for some years after the war ended and, in due course, some found their way to the Syrian Army, with which they served on the Golan Heights until the Six Day War of 1967.

MATILDA (INFANTRY TANK Mk II (A12))

Weight: 26.5 tons
Speed: 15mph
Armour: 78mm
Armament: one 2pdr gun (or one 3in howitzer on close support models), one Vickers .303in machine-gun (Mk I); replaced by one Besa 7.92mm machine-gun on subsequent marks
Engines: Mks I and II two AEC 87hp diesel; Mks III–V two Leyland 95hp diesel
Crew: 4.

Strictly speaking, the name Matilda belonged not to the A12 but to its diminutive two-man predecessor the Infantry Tank Mk I (A11), the strange appearance of which reminded the then Master-General of the Ordnance, Major-General Hugh Elles, who had commanded the Tank Corps during the First World War, of a cartoon duck of the same name. The A11 was protected by 60mm armour, which was impressive by the standards of the mid-1930s, but its armament of one machine-gun was obviously inadequate and design work quickly began on the larger A12, the specification for which included a 2pdr gun for use against enemy tanks and a coaxial machine-gun. The prototype A12 was produced by the Vulcan Foundry of Warrington in 1938 and production commenced the following year. By association, the A12 was known as Matilda

Above: Matilda Is training with the BEF in France during the winter of 1939/40. Despite its strange appearance, the tank performed well during the Arras counter-attack. (IWM)

Below: Matilda IIs of 7 RTR at a forward rally point during the taking of the Sidi Barrani fortified camps, December 1940. (IWM)

II for a while, the II being dropped when the A11 was phased out in 1940.

The Matilda (A12) was a soundly engineered vehicle, although it did not lend itself to mass production. It did, however, differ from many contemporary designs in that it dispensed with a frame and instead employed heavy, specially shaped armoured castings welded into a rigid hull structure, together with a cast turret and mantlet and thick skirting plates which protected the bell-crank coil-spring suspension bogies. Further advantages included power traverse and the twin engines, one of which generated just sufficient power to take the vehicle to safety if the other were out of action. Deficiencies

in the design included the fact that it could not be up-gunned, the heavy wear on its steering clutches and the vulnerability of its turret ring, which could be jammed by shell splinters. Nevertheless, at the time it was introduced the Matilda's main armour was invulnerable to every German and Italian tank, anti-tank or field artillery weapon in service and because of this the vehicle was known for a while as The Queen of the Battlefield.

On 21 May 1940 the 58 A11s and sixteen A12s of 1 Army Tank Brigade spearheaded a critical counter-attack by elements of 50th (Northumbrian) Division at Arras, cutting Rommel's 7th Panzer Division in two for a while and creating a situation in which it

was possible to plan the successful evacuation from Dunkirk. Later that year the 7th Royal Tank Regiment, equipped with Matilda IIs, was dispatched to Egypt, which had been invaded by a large Italian army. At Sidi Barrani, and again at Bardia and Tobruk, the invulnerable Matildas smashed through the enemy defences and carried all before them, to the delight of the infantry they were supporting. This immunity ended in the spring of 1941 with the arrival of the Africa Corps' dual-purpose Eighty-Eights. Matildas nevertheless took part in every major desert battle until mid-1942 and played an important role in effecting a junction between the Eighth Army and the besieged garrison of Tobruk during Operation 'Crusader'. After many had been lost during the fighting at Gazala it was recognized that the vehicle was no longer suitable for employment as a gun tank in the Middle East theatre of war and it fought its last action in this role during the First Battle of Alamein. In

smaller numbers, Matildas were also employed in Eritrea, Crete and Malta, and some were sent to the Soviet Union. In Australian hands, however, the Matilda continued to serve as a gun tank in the Far East, where the anti-tank capability of the Japanese was well below that of the Germans, fighting further battles in New Guinea, Bougainville and Borneo.

Among the special-purpose vehicles based on the Matilda was an armoured searchlight, known for security purposes as a Canal Defence Light (CDL). This employed a specially designed turret containing a high-intensity arc light and two reflectors, the beam passing through a vertical slit across which a steel shutter was oscillated to produce a dazzle effect. Power for the light projector was supplied by the tank's main engines. By 1942 two Matilda CDL regiments were present in the Middle East, but had not completed their training in time to take part in the Second Battle of Alamein. In due course the Grant was

standardized as the principal CDL mounting and small numbers were used operationally in 1945 during the Rhine and Elbe crossings. Some mention has been made earlier of the Scorpion flail, a few of which were employed at Second Alamein. The Australian Army also developed the Frog flamethrower, which had a range of 100 yards.

A total of 2,987 Matildas were built, production ceasing in August 1943. The Matilda's part in the destruction of the Italian Army during the Western Desert fighting of 1940–1 earned it a unique distinction in the history of armoured warfare in that it remains to this day the only tank design to have contributed in so large a measure to a strategic victory, despite the fact that for much of the time it was employed in little more than squadron strength.

T-34/76 AND T-34/85

T-34/76
Weight: 26.3 tons
Speed: 31mph
Armour: 45mm
Armament: one 76.2mm L/30.5 gun; two 7.62mm machine-guns
Engine: V-2-34 500hp diesel
Crew: 4.
(Specification for Model 40 (German designation T-34/76A))

T-34/85
Weight: 32 tons
Speed: 31mph
Armour: 60mm
Armament: one 85mm L/53 gun; two 7.62mm machine-guns
Engine: V-2-34 500hp diesel
Crew: 5.

Because of its excellent balance between mobility, protection and firepower, the T-34 Series is widely regarded as being the starting-point of modern tank design. It was evolved by the design team headed by Mikhail Koshkin at the Kharkov Locomotive Works as a replacement for the Soviet BT cruiser tank series, which were fast but thinly armoured, and incorporated features from several intermediate designs, including the A20, A30 and T-32. The T-34 was driven by a reliable V-2 12-cylinder 500hp diesel engine, giving an excellent power-to-weight ratio. Like the BTs, the vehicle employed the Christie big-wheel high-speed suspension, and to this were added wide tracks which enabled it to remain mobile in mud or snow; this mobility in conditions which German tanks found extreme difficulty in operating at all earned it the nickname of The Snow King. Another feature inherited from the BTs was the means of transferring drive to the tracks. Instead of a conventional toothed sprocket a recessed wheel was employed, rollers in the recesses engaging alternate lugs on the track. No retaining device was required to secure the track-pins, which were round-headed and inserted from the inside; if the pins worked loose they were knocked back into place by a curved wiper plate welded to the hull. The hull itself overhung the tracks and had sloped sides, while the 45mm glacis plate was laid back at an angle of 45 degrees, giving the same ballistic protection as 90mm plate in the vertical plane without paying the penalty of increased weight. Finally, the 76.2mm L/30.5 gun was capable of penetrating every German tank in service at the time the design was conceived, the choice of weapon having been influenced by a mistaken belief that the Germans were employing much thicker armour that was in fact the case.

Apart from the provision of intercom and electric power traverse, driven from the vehicle batteries, the T-34 was almost totally lacking in the sort of sophisticated equipment to be found in Western and German tanks. On the other hand, it was simple, robust and soldier-proof, all qualities that enabled crews to be trained quickly in its use. The early models, however, did have a number of defects which affected the operational performance of the vehicle. It was, for example, a mistake to opt for a two-man turret when better results could be obtained with a

Right: The T-34/76 provided an excellent balance between firepower, protection and mobility and is widely regarded as being the start-point of modern tank design. This example is a Model 40, armed with a 76.2mm L/30.5 gun.

Below: The neat hole between the two exhausts indicate that this T-34/76 Model 40 has been knocked out from the rear. The German tank guns of 1941 were incapable of penetrating the vehicle's frontal or side armour. (RAC Tank Museum)

turret crew consisting of commander, gunner and loader. As it was, the commander also acted as gunner and the loader was required to handle ammunition in impossibly cramped conditions. Furthermore, the earliest models were fitted with a one-piece turret hatch that opened forward in the manner of a suitcase lid, impeding vision, and when closed down visual aids for the commander were reduced to one episcope and the gunsight, and for the loader to one episcope.

The prototype T-34/76 was completed in January 1940 and mass production commenced in June of that year. The Model 41 of 1941 was up-gunned with a more powerful 76.2mm L/41.2, as was the Model 42, which also incorporated several less important modifications; both of these versions were referred to by the Germans as the T-34/76B. The Model 43 saw the introduction of a re-designed hexagonal turret with two roof hatches and, later, a commander's cupola. This version, known to the Germans as T-34/76C, entered service in late 1942 and remained in production until the end of 1945; an improved model with 110mm frontal armour is sometimes referred to as the T-43.

The shock engendered by the Wehrmacht's first encounters with the T-34/76 was such that, for a short period, it gave serious consideration to copying the design and putting it straight into production. There were, however, technical difficulties involved in producing aluminium components for the diesel engine, as well as a degree of reluctance to admit in so open a fashion that the despised Russians were capable of producing a superior design. Instead, the German Army was forced to embark on a hasty programme of up-armouring and up-gunning existing tanks and assault guns, producing a fleet of interim tank destroyers, accelerating the introduction of the Tiger E

Above: The T-34/76 Models 41 and 42 were up-gunned with the longer (L/41.2) version of the 76.2mm weapon. The photograph shows a set-piece attack in the Ukraine. (Novosti)

Left: The T-34/76 Model 43 saw the introduction of a roomier hexagonal turret. Later versions such as this were also fitted with a commander's cupola. (RAC Tank Museum)

Right: The T-34/85 was fitted with a specially designed three-man turret although basic T-34 hull and chassis were retained. (RAC Tank Museum)

and commencing design work on the Panther.

By 1943 most of these measures had begun to take effect and the T-34/76 had lost something of its qualitative edge. The implications of this latest twist in the gun/armour spiral were immediately apparent and in the summer of 1943 it was decided that the T-34 would itself be up-gunned with the same 85mm weapon that armed the KV85 and the SU-85. As the old turret had reached the limit of its development potential a larger three-man turret was designed, although the basic T-34 hull and chassis were retained. The T-34/85 entered service in the spring of 1944 and was issued to independent tank brigades.

Almost 40,000 T-34s were built from 1940 to 1945. They continued to be built in the immediate post-war years and saw further active service in the Korean War, the Arab/Israeli Wars and many other conflicts. Some are still on the strength of the armies of the Soviet Union's Third World clients.

PANZERKAMPF-WAGEN V PANTHER

Weight: 43–45.5 tons
Speed: 34mph
Armour: 120mm
Armament: one 75mm L/70 gun; two 7.92mm machine-guns
Engine: Maybach HL230/P30 700hp petrol
Crew: 5.

The German Army entered the Second World War without a second generation of tanks on its drawing-boards and was, therefore, caught seriously short in its first encounters with the Soviet T-34/76. It appreciated that while its expedient solutions, some of which have been described above, would suffice for the moment, the long-term answer could only lie in the production of a new medium tank that was better armed than the T-34/76, had comparable armour arrangement and was capable of a good cross-country performance. On 25 November 1941 the Heereswaffenamt, responsible for procure-

ment, issued a competitive specification which provided for initially a 75mm L/48, then a 75mm L/70 main armament, a 30–35ton weight range and a maximum speed of 35mph.

Daimler-Benz and Maschinefabrik Augsburg-Nürnberg (MAN) both tendered for the project and had their plans ready by the spring of 1942. Hitler's personal preference was for the Daimler-Benz candidate, until it was pointed out that its similarity to the T-34/76 was too close for

Below: The Panther was rushed through its development process and was committed to action prematurely. Once its various faults had been cured it became the best medium tank design of the war. The photograph shows a Model D and emphasizes the clean lines of the design. (RAC Tank Museum)

comfort and that as a result of the turret being mounted so far forward the main armament overhang protruded an unacceptable distance ahead of the vehicle. The MAN candidate, which copied only the T-34's glacis, laid back at the steeper angle of 35 degrees, was therefore accepted. The vehicle followed the conventional German layout and line of drive to the forward sprockets, but was carried on an interleaved eight-bogie suspension employing an internal torsion bar system which increased the tank's height but gave an excellent ride. Main armament overhang had been reduced by siting the turret well back.

By the time the first Panthers, designated Model D, began leaving the production lines early in 1943 it had been decided to increase the armour basis to 80mm on the glacis and 120mm on the mantlet. The tank's weight was already in excess of the original specification and the effect of these further modifications was to increase it to

45 tons. To compensate this the powerful Maybach HL230/P30 engine was fitted. The combined result was a technical nightmare as transmission components and steering linkages, intended for use in a vehicle 30 per cent lighter, failed when subjected to the heavier stresses imposed by a combination of increased weight and power; furthermore, the engine was prone to overheating and petrol fires broke out regularly. This was the inevitable penalty of rushing a design straight into production and time was needed to correct the faults. Time, however, was not available for Hitler who, contrary to the advice of General Heinz Guderian, the Inspector-General of Armoured Troops, insisted that the vehicle be committed to action during the assault on the Kursk Salient in July. At the end of the first day's fighting 160 of the 200

Panthers on the strength of Fourth Panzer Army were out of action, the majority with mechanical problems, and many of these were irretrievably lost when the Soviet Army mounted its counter-offensive.

Work was already in hand on modifications that would cure the various faults and these were incorporated in the second production version, the Model A, which appeared shortly after Kursk. This version also saw the introduction of a ball mounting for the hull machine-gun, this having been previously fired through a hinged flap in the glacis, and an improved commander's cupola. The Model G entered service in the spring of 1944 and dispensed with the driver's vision hatch in the glacis in favour of a rotating episcope in the roof of the driving compartment; in addition, internal space had been gained by fitting the upper-

Above: Allied troops examine a Panther captured in Italy. A stowage rack for jerricans has been welded to the rear of the engine deck. (RAC Tank Museum)

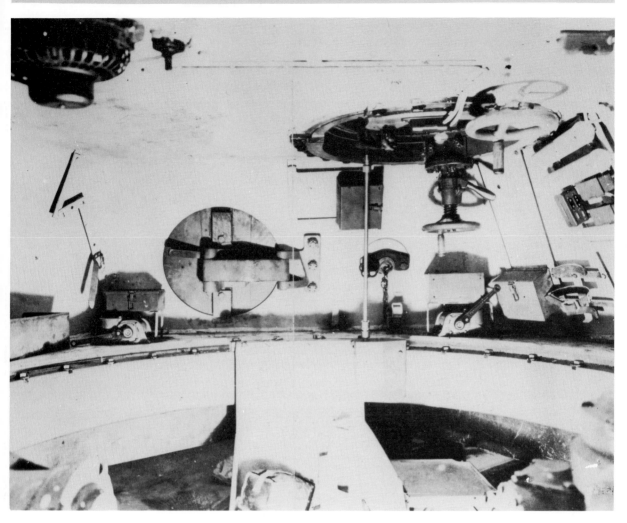

Above: Interior rear face of Panther Model D turret. In the centre are the circular escape hatch and the drive shaft linking the cupola's counter-rotating clock scale with the turret rack. On the right are the handwheel controlling the position of the vision-block mantlet and the cupola hatch elevating handwheel with the position lever above. (RAC Tank Museum)

hull side plates at a less oblique angle. Altogether, 5,508 Panthers were built, of which 3,740 were Model Gs.

Once the Panther's teething troubles had been cured it settled down to become the best medium tank design of the war, equipping one of the panzer regiment's two battalions. Its frontal armour was proof against the Soviet 122mm gun at ranges above 900 metres; against the British 17pdr, the American 90mm and the Soviet 85mm above 600 metres; and against the British and American 75mm and the Soviet 76.2mm L/41.5 above 500 metres; the British 6pdr failed to achieve complete penetration at 300 metres. Against flank and rear shots the vehicle became vulnerable at much greater ranges, from 3,500 metres in the case of the Soviet 122mm to 500 metres in the case of the

British 6pdr. It was possible to deflect a shot from the underside of the curved mantlet through the thin roof of the driving compartment, and the fact that latterly the mantlet was re-designed with a flatter profile suggests that this took place more often than was generally realized. Likewise, an AP round could be bounced off hard ground immediately in front of the vehicle in the hope that it would ricochet through the belly plates, but this required exceptional skill, courage and luck.

The Panther's 75mm L/70 gun was capable of penetrating the frontal armour of the Russian IS Series at 600 metres, the Churchill and the T-34 at 800 metres and the Sherman at 1,000 metres. Like the L/48 gun of the Pz Kpfw IV it was muzzle heavy and this was compensated by linking it to a small hydraulic cylinder located on the

right of the mounting. When out of use the weapon could be locked horizontally by an internal crutch, but for rail transits or long road marches it would be rested on a hinged external barrel clamp mounted on the roof of the driving compartment. A two-speed hydraulic power traverse system was fitted, power being drawn from the main drive shaft through a fluid coupling, and the commander and gunner were equipped with gun- and target-position indicators similar to those installed in the Pz Kpfw IV.

Despite numerous modifications which included the installation of an automatic fire-extinguisher in the engine compartment, the automotive aspects remained the weakest point in the Panther's design and it was accepted that a complete overhaul would be required every 450–600 miles. Areas that continued to cause concern were the gearbox, which would not tolerate heavy handling, particularly in the vital lower-middle range, and an inherent weakness in the reduction drives to the drive sprockets, which were under-tensioned for the torque they had to transmit. The final drive assembly incorporated the same complex controlled-differential steering that was installed in the Tigers and the Churchill. This was extremely efficient but contained an immanent danger in that if the steering levers were touched while the engine was running and the gearbox in neutral the result was the 'neutral turn', in which the tank began turning within its own axis, with potentially fatal consequences for anyone standing nearby.

A projected Panther II, which might have been armed with an 88mm gun, was completed as far as the hull prototype stage but was later abandoned. The Panther's most notable derivative was the Jagdpanther tank destroyer, but command, artillery observation post and recovery versions were also produced. During the Italian campaign Panther turrets on ground mountings were built into the defences of the Hitler and Gothic Lines; they were almost impossible to spot as they lay only inches above the ground, were expertly camouflaged, and only opened fire at the last minute in the certain knowledge of a kill.

PANZERKAMPF-WAGEN VI TIGER

Tiger E
Weight: 55 tons
Speed: 23mph
Armour: 100mm
Armament: one 88mm L/56 gun; two 7.92mm machine-guns
Engine: Maybach HL230 V-12 700hp petrol
Crew: 5.

Tiger B
Weight: 68.7 tons
Speed: 23.5mph
Armour: 150mm
Armament: one 88mm L/71 gun; two 7.92mm machine-guns
Engine: Maybach HL230/P30 700hp petrol
Crew: 5.

The Tiger E lay outside the mainstream of German tank development in that it represented the consolidation of a series of competitive designs which stemmed from a pre-war requirement for a heavy breakthrough tank. Work on these continued slowly, but in May 1941 the Heereswaffenamt issued a revised specification calling for an 88mm main armament and an overall weight of 45 tons. This decision was taken as a result of the Panzerwaffe's experience against the French Char Bs and the British Matildas, but was none the less remarkable in that it was made one month before the invasion of the Soviet Union and without foreknow-ledge of the qualities possessed by the Russian T-34/76 and KV Series. The Porsche and Henschel organizations had their designs ready to demonstrate to the Führer at Rastenburg on his birthday, 20 April 1942, and, despite being more than 10 tons heavier than the specification, the Henschel machine was adjudged the superior; as described elsewhere, the Porsche candidate found employment as the Elefant heavy tank destroyer.

Production commenced in August 1942, the tank's official designation being Pz Kpfw VI Tiger Model H, renamed Pz Kpfw VI Tiger E in 1944, by which title the vehicle is generally known. An interleaved torsion bar suspension was employed in conjunction with wide tracks, although this increased the overall width to the point at which rail transit was impossible. A narrow track was therefore supplied for use on rail flats, the outer wheels being removed from each bogie when it was fitted. Because of the tank's weight a simple clutch-and-brake steering mechanism was considered unsuitable. Instead, a hydraulic regenerative controlled-differential steering unit was employed; this produced such positive response and was so light that it was possible to control direction with two fingers on the steering wheel. If the power steering failed, the driver could in emergency resort to two steering levers which acted on the vehicle brakes. Further automotive points of interest were the

Maybach Olvar pre-selector gearbox, giving eight forward and four reverse gears, and the inertia starter which could be used in severe weather or instead of the electric self-starter system if the vehicle batteries were run down.

The Tiger E's armour (100mm on the front plate, 110mm on the mantlet and 60–80mm on the side) betrayed its pre-war origins by the number of vertical surfaces it presented, but its sheer bulk sufficed. The 122mm gun of the Soviet IS series, which relied on the weight and mass of its round as much as the muzzle velocity with which it was fired, was capable of defeating the frontal armour, but only at ranges at which the Russian tanks were themselves vulnerable. The various tank guns of the Western Allies, however, were not, although they could penetrate the side and rear. The British 6pdr could penetrate the side armour at 500 metres, the British and American 75mm at 700 metres, the 3in gun of the M10 at 1,400 metres, and the British

Above: Rear view of the same vehicle undergoing trials in the United Kingdom, showing details of the Feifel air filter system installed for running in permanently dusty climates. (RAC Tank Museum)

Right: The sheer bulk of the Tiger E provides a dramatic contrast with the diminutive Valentine alongside.

17pdr and American 90mm at 1,900 metres.

In sharp contrast, the Tiger E's 88mm gun was capable of destroying Allied medium tanks at 3,000 metres, and heavier designs including the Churchill, M26 Pershing and IS II at somewhat shorter ranges. The gun itself was muzzle-heavy, this being corrected in the usual way by a linkage to a balance spring in a cylinder bolted to the right quadrant of the turret ring. The turret weighed 20 tons and although the gunner's hand traverse was geared its use involved such heavy labour that it was linked to an auxiliary handwheel turned by the commander. A two-speed power traverse was also available, driven from the main drive shaft by means of a hydraulic coupling. Gun- and target-position indicators were fitted for the commander and gunner, as well as a clinometer for the latter.

A total of 1,350 Tiger Es were built before production was terminated in August 1944. The vehicle had a premature and

Below: Despite its unscientific arrangement, the Tiger E's frontal armour was virtually impenetrable. Often, as in this case, only a flank shot would serve to immobilize the vehicle. (RAC Tank Museum)

Top left: Driving compartment of Tiger E, showing steering wheel, instrument panel and gear selector lever; spare vision blocks are stowed above the instruments. (RAC Tank Museum)

Left: Tiger E commander's position showing auxiliary traverse handwheel and the cupola clock scale drive shaft. (RAC Tank Museum)

Above: The first 50 Tiger Bs were completed with round-fronted Porsche turrets which could deflect shot down through the thinner roof armour of the driving compartment. (RAC Tank Museum)

unfortunate baptism of fire near Leningrad in August 1942 and continued to serve on the Eastern Front for the duration of the war, as well as in Tunisia, Sicily, Italy, France and north-west Europe, equipping heavy tank battalions which were usually at the disposal of panzer corps commanders. Command and recovery versions were produced, but the only special-purpose derivative was the Sturmtiger, a heavy assault gun armed with a 380mm rocket-launcher. This fired a 761lb spin-stabilized demolition charge to a range of 6,000 yards, but by the time it appeared in 1944 the German Army was wholly engaged in defensive battles and, since the need for such a vehicle had long passed, only a handful were built.

Even as the Tiger E entered service, plans were put into effect to produce an even better-protected model with a still larger gun, thereby giving Germany a decisive advantage in the gun/armour spiral. Once more, Henschel and Porsche were asked to submit competitive designs and again the Henschel candidate was

successful. The vehicle had a conventional layout and was standardized as the Pz Kpfw VI Tiger Model B, and was sometimes referred to as the Tiger II, although it was known popularly in Germany as the Königstiger (King Tiger) and among the Allies as the Royal Tiger. Production commenced in February 1943.

At 68.7 tons the Tiger B was the heaviest tank to enter general service during the Second World War. Its armour (150mm on the glacis, 185mm on the turret front and 80mm on the side) was arranged more scientifically than that of the Tiger E and was angled between 20 and 25 degrees. The choice of the 88mm L/71 KwK 43 gun as main armament set the designers the problems, first, of installing so large a weapon in a turret capable of all-round traverse and, secondly, of handling the long, heavy rounds of ammunition in a confined space. It was, too, immediately apparent that not only was the weapon muzzle-heavy in its mounting, but that its sheer weight would throw the turret out of balance and cause it to bear down on its

leading edge. These problems were ingeniously solved by building out the front of the turret, leaving a gap of 14½ inches between the interior of the turret front plate and the inside of the turret ring. This enabled the trunnions to be fitted well forward and so provided the loader with sufficient room in which to work; to compensate the frontal weight a turret bustle was added to the rear, holding 22 rounds of main armament ammunition. Muzzle-heaviness was corrected by means of a hydro-pneumatic cylinder, installed to the right of the mounting.

The first fifty vehicles to be completed were fitted with turrets that had already been built by Porsche; these, unfortunately, had rounded fronts which could deflect shots through the roof of the driving compartment. The standard Henschel turret was flat-fronted with a slight backwards slope and this, together with a heavy bell mantlet, eliminated the danger. While superficially similar to the Tiger E suspension, that of the Tiger B employed overlapping as opposed to interleaved bogie units, because this system proved less vulnerable to compacted stones and earth, which could cause wheel jamming. In other respects the Tiger B followed the pattern of the Tiger E, with numerous minor improvements. Tiger Bs began leaving the production lines in February 1944. A total of 484 were built, serving alongside the Tiger Es in the heavy tank battalions. A command version was produced as well as the Jagdtiger heavy tank destroyer, mention of which has already been made.

It was freely admitted by Allied tank experts that in terms of firepower and protection the Tigers represented a considerable advance on anything the Allies had available. On the other hand, their weight, size and heavy fuel consumption imposed serious limits on their mobility. Again, while they earned themselves a fearsome reputation, inflicted devastating casualties on their opponents and won most of their battles, they failed to influence the outcome of a single campaign. This, coupled with the fact that each Tiger cost 800,000 Reichsmarks and required 300,000 man-hours to complete,

raises the question of whether scarce materials and resources would not have been better employed in constructing simpler designs.

MEDIUM TANK M4 (SHERMAN)

Weight: 30.2–33.6 tons
Speed: 24–29mph
Armour: 75–105mm
Armament: one 75mm gun; two .30cal Browning machine-guns
Engine(s):one Wright Continental R-975 petrol radial 353hp (M4/M4A1); two General Motors 6-71 diesel, each 187.5hp (M4A2); one Ford GAA V-8 petrol 500hp (M4A3); five Chrysler WC Multibank petrol, total 370hp (M4A4); one Caterpillar RD-1820 diesel radial 450hp (M4A6)
Crew: 5.

The M4 was designed as the standard medium tank of the United States Army and replaced the stop-gap Medium Tank M3 Lee, although it inherited the latter's proven chassis, engine, transmission and lower hull. However, while the M3's 75mm main armament had been housed in a sponson on the right side of the hull and supplemented by a 37mm gun in a top turret, the M4 mounted its 75mm gun in a conventional cast turret with all-round traverse and dispensed with the 37mm altogether. A trials vehicle, the T6, also incorporated the M3's sponson doors but these were omitted when the M4 design was standardized on 5 September 1941. The prototype was completed by the Lima Locomotive Works in February 1942. Mass production commenced the following month and involved ten major manufacturers, including the American Locomotive Company, Baldwin Locomotive Works, Chrysler Detroit Tank Arsenal, Federal Machine and Welder Company, Fisher Grand Blanc Arsenal, Ford Motor Company, Lima Locomotive Works, Pacific

Left: The Sherman first saw action with the British Eighth Army during the Second Battle of Alamein, the models employed being the M4, the M4A1 and the M4A2. The photograph shows a Sherman of the 4th County of London Yeomanry, then serving with 23 Armoured Brigade, crossing a causeway over the Wadi Akarit anti-tank ditch during the advance into Tunisia. (IWM)

Below: The M4A1 employed a cast hull and was the first model to enter mass production, 6,281 being built. (USAMHI)

Car & Foundry Company, Pressed Steel Car Company and Pullman Standard Manufacturing Company. When production ceased in June 1945 no fewer than 49,234 had been built, exceeding the combined tank output of the United Kingdom and Germany; a further 188 M4A1s were built in Canada under the name of Grizzly I. The principal differences between the various models lay in the power units they employed, although the M4A1 was easily identified by its cast as opposed to welded hull. The Canadian Ram medium tank was broadly similar in design to the M4 and was designated M4A5 by the US Ordnance Department.

Active service revealed two major deficiencies in the design. The first was that the Sherman was seriously undergunned in comparison with the Tiger and Panther and from January 1944 later models of the M4A1, M4A2 and M4A3 were armed with a longer 76mm gun mounted in a larger turret, adding the suffix (76) to their designation; this provided some improvement although its performance fell below that of the British Firefly conversion, which was armed with a 17pdr gun. Secondly, if the vehicle were penetrated fire spread so quickly that the enemy called it The Ronson or The Tommy Cooker. In an attempt to contain this, wet stowage was

Below: Sherman M4A1 (76) of the 6th South African Armoured Division taking part in the advance on Bologna, 1945. The larger gun required a re-designed turret. (SANMMHI)

adopted for the ammunition, which was re-housed in water-protected racks beneath the turret floor. Models so equipped, including the M4A1(76), M4A2(76), M4A3 and M4A3(76), added W to their designation. Close-support versions of the M4 and M4A3, armed with a 105mm howitzer, were also produced in 1944, adding (105) to their designation. The last version to enter service, the M4A3E2, was designed as an assault tank and was protected by 150mm armour which increased the weight to 42 tons.

The basic Sherman suspension was first used on the M2 and M3 medium tanks and consisted of three two-wheel bogie units per side incorporating vertical volute springs in each assembly. The steady increase in the tank's weight, however, led to the introduction of the horizontal volute spring suspension (HVSS), which was used in conjunction with wider tracks on some models from the middle of 1944 onwards.

American ordnance designations were not used by the British Army, which referred to the various models as follows: M4 – Sherman I; M4A1 – Sherman II; M4A2 – Sherman III; M4A3 – Sherman IV; M4A4 – Sherman V. Where appropriate, the following suffixes were added: A – 76mm gun; B – 105mm howitzer; C – 17pdr gun; Y – HVSS. The Sherman VC was thus a Firefly conversion based on the M4A4.

The thickness of the Sherman's armour had been decided during the period that the German Army was still using comparatively small tank and anti-tank guns. By the time the vehicle entered service, therefore, it was becoming increasingly vulnerable. In Europe some American units sought to provide additional protection by stacking layers of sandbags on the glacis or against the hull sides, the latter being held in place by welded rails. The inevitable penalty of adding so much extra weight was reduced mobility.

Internally, the Sherman contained a number of interesting points. An

Left: A Sherman platoon of the US 755th Tank Battalion employed in the supplementary artillery role during the Italian campaign. (USAMHI)

emergency escape hatch was positioned in the floor immediately behind the hull gunner's seat and an auxiliary generator, located in the left rear of the fighting compartment, was used not only for battery charging but also to heat the engine compartment in cold weather, thereby assisting starting. Power traverse, which could be either hydraulically or electrically operated, was available to the commander and gunner, the final lay being made by the gunner with a handwheel. The gun itself was fitted with a gyro-stabilizer, although this controlled its movements in elevation only. A traverse indicator and clinometer made indirect shooting possible and in static conditions the vehicle was often used in the supplementary artillery role.

The Sherman first saw action during the Second Battle of Alamein after 300 had been withdrawn from American units in training and shipped to the hard-pressed Eighth Army in Egypt. It subsequently served in every major theatre of war and, as well as providing the backbone of the US Armored Force, was supplied to the majority of America's allies, including the Soviet Union. Its derivatives included the Sherman DD, the Crab flail tank, self-propelled artillery mountings and tank destroyers, the Calliope and Whiz-Bang

multi-barrel rocket-launcher systems, the Skink anti-aircraft tank, a mine roller, and many experimental projects. Since 1945 the Sherman has seen further active service in Korea, the Middle East and India and, in much altered form, remains active in some armies to this day.

Above: The Sherman Firefly was armed with the British 17pdr gun. This example, belonging to the 1st Krechowiecki Lancers (II Polish Corps), is seen crossing a Churchill Ark during the final stages of the campaign in Italy. (Sikorski Museum)

CHURCHILL (INFANTRY TANK MK IV (A22))

Weight: Mks I and II 38.5 tons; Mks III to VI 39 tons; Mks VII and VIII 40 tons

Speed: 15.5mph (Mks VII and VIII 12.5mph)

Armour: Mks I to VI 102mm; Mks VII and VIII 152mm

Armament:

Mk I: one 2pdr gun in turret; one 3in howitzer in front plate; one 7.92mm machine-gun

Mk II: one 3in howitzer in front plate; one 2pdr gun in ~~front plate~~ turret; one 7.92mm machine-gun

Mks III and IV: one 6pdr gun; two 7.92mm machine-guns

Mk IV (NA75): one 75mm gun ex-Sherman; one .30cal coaxial machine-gun; one 7.92mm machine-gun in hull

Mk V: one 95mm howitzer; two 7.92mm machine-guns

Mk VI: one 75mm gun; two 7.92mm machine-guns

Mk VII: one 75mm gun; two 7.92mm machine-guns

Mk VIII: one 95mm howitzer; two 7.92mm machine-guns

Engine: Bedford Twin-Six 350hp petrol
Crew: 5.

In 1939 many British senior officers believed that the fighting in France would resemble the later battles of 1918 and requested pilot models of a heavy infantry tank with a wide trench-crossing capability and the capacity to cross the worst shell-torn ground. The project was designated A20 and the prototypes were evaluated shortly after the Dunkirk evacuation. As the Army was desperately short of tanks it was decided to build a scaled-down version which would retain the same engine as the A20. This was officially known as the A22

Below: Cutaway of the Churchill Mk I, armed with a 2pdr gun in the turret and a 3in howitzer in the bow. (RAC Tank Museum)

but was named Churchill in the interests of morale. Vauxhall Motors Ltd. were made responsible for the project and were able to meet a request that the vehicle should enter production within one year. Teething troubles were numerous, but, in contrast to the Panther's early troubled history, these were solved by constant modification and improvement and the tank was mechanically reliable by the time it went into action in 1942.

As can be seen from the specifications above, the Churchill carried a wider variety of armament than any other British tank design. Mks I and II were attempts to provide a balanced armour-piercing/high-explosive capability, because the 2pdr did not fire HE ammunition at the time they were produced. Subsequent developments involved up-gunning the vehicle with the 6pdr and then the 75mm, while Mks V and VIII, armed with a 95mm howitzer, were produced for the close-support role. High-explosive ammunition was not available for the 6pdr in North Africa, although the deficiency was remedied during the Italian campaign, and this led to the ingenious conversion known as the NA75 (North Africa 75mm), devised

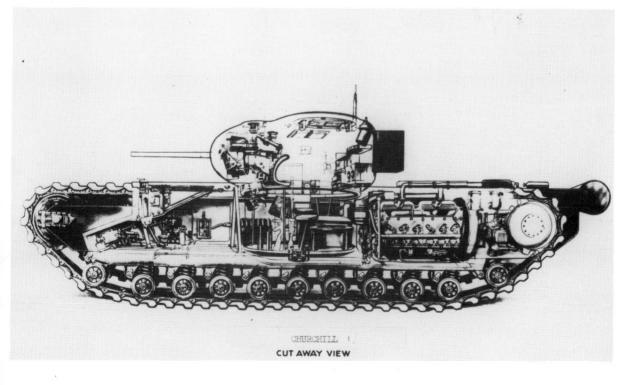

CHURCHILL I
CUT AWAY VIEW

Left: Chuchill Mk IV of 48 RTR passing an AVRE, Italy 1945. Early models of the Mk IV were fitted with a prominent counter-weight on the muzzle of the 6pdr. (IWM)

Below: The Churchill Mk V was a close support tank armed with a 95mm howitzer, fitted with a heavy counter-weight. (RAC Tank Museum)

Above: Infantry and Churchills of 'A' Squadron, 7 RTR attack through the ground mist of a Normandy dawn. The Mk VI version of the Churchill was the first to be armed with the British 75mm gun. (IWM)

Below: One of the Churchill's least attractive characteristics was its air-flow system. When the vehicle was stationary on hard, dusty ground its powerful sirocco fan would raise a dust storm under the tank's belly, then suck it in through the hatches; unless the latter were closed promptly, everything within would be quickly covered with a gritty patina. In Tunisia canvas aprons were used to correct this, but these do not seem to have been issued in other theatres. (IWM)

by REME officer, Major Percy Morrell, in which 200 Mk IVs were fitted with dual-capability AP/HE 75mm guns stripped from damaged Shermans. The British 75mm represented the limit of the design's potential, however, and it remained under-gunned throughout its career. A variety of turrets were employed, all of them cast with the exception of that of the Mk III, which was of welded construction. One version of the original A20 specification was to have been armed with two 2pdr guns housed in sponsons in the manner of the First World War tanks and the hull escape hatches were a legacy of this. The suspension consisted of 22 independently sprung small-diameter bogies which could be removed and replaced as separate units. A four-speed Merritt-Brown gearbox pro-vided controlled-differential steering, imposed by means of a tiller bar. While badly arranged, the tank's armour proved capable of absorbing tremendous punish-ment.

Churchills first went into action with the Canadian Calgary Regiment at Dieppe on 19 August 1942, and six took part in the Second Battle of Alamein with a trials unit named Kingforce. Two Churchill-equipped tank brigades provided infantry support in Tunisia and, later, in Italy. Three such tank

brigades fought in Normandy and north-west Europe, one being converted to the Crocodile role. Sufficient Churchills were also sent to the Soviet Union to equip at least one heavy tank regiment. In action the vehicle fully vindicated its designers' concept of mobility. It was capable of scaling slopes so steep that the enemy considered them tank-proof, coped with the earth banks of the Normandy bocage without apparent difficulty, and in the Reichswald ploughed through deep mud which brought other tracked vehicles to a standstill.

Together, the Churchill's mobility and its roomy hull rendered it suitable for coversion to a wide variety of assault engineering roles some of which, including the AVRE, the Ark and the Crocodile, have already been mentioned. There was also a turretless bridgelayer which employed hydraulic arms to launch a 30-foot 60-ton capacity bridge over the front of the vehicle; these were initially issued at brigade level, but by the end of the war most Churchill regiments had several on strength. Other developments included a primitive assault gun, hastily produced for home defence in 1941, and numerous experimental projects. A total of 5,640 Churchills were built.

Above: The Churchill Mk VII was protected by 152mm armour and could be identified by its round sponson escape doors. The Mk VIII was a close-support version armed with a 95mm howitzer. (RAC Tank Museum)

3. Tanks at War

MINOR TACTICS OF THE TANK BATTLE

Figure 1 shows a tank in the turret-down position. The vehicle is concealed behind a crest which also protects it from direct gunfire, but the commander can still observe to his front.

Figure 2 shows a tank in the hull-down position. The vehicle's turret is now visible to the enemy but its hull is still protected by the crest and it can itself engage. Whenever terrain permitted, hull-down was adopted as the normal fighting position.

Figure 3 shows a three-tank troop jockeying on a crest-line during an engagement. On average, three rounds were needed to acquire and destroy a target at anything other than point-blank range. It was logical, therefore, to assume that the enemy employed similar gunnery techniques and to upset his aim the tanks change their position frequently by reversing below the crest and coming up at a different place.

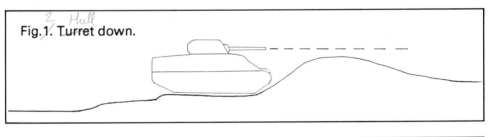

Fig.1. Turret down.

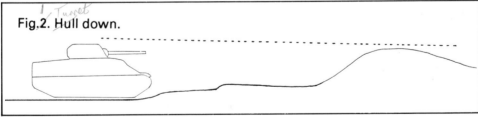

Fig.2. Hull down.

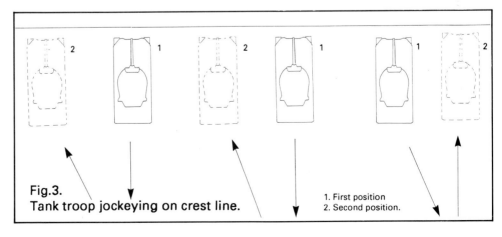

Fig.3.
Tank troop jockeying on crest line.

1. First position
2. Second position.

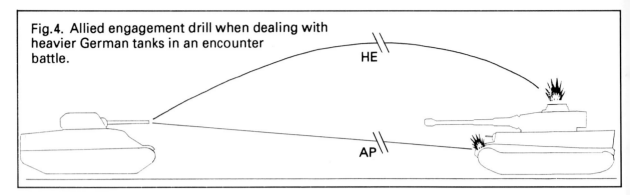

Fig.4. Allied engagement drill when dealing with heavier German tanks in an encounter battle.

HE

AP

Figure 4 demonstrates a technique often used by Allied tank commanders in sudden encounters with heavier German tanks. First a round of high-explosive was burst on the enemy's turret; this would not penetrate the armour, but the explosion could temporarily disorient the commander and smash his vision devices. Next, an armour-piercing round would be used to shatter one of the enemy's tracks unless the target was in such close proximity that the armour was itself vulnerable. Having thus immobilized his opponent and gained a temporary respite, the Allied commander would reverse out of trouble while other tanks attempted to manoeuvre against the enemy's flank. The flank shot (**Figure 5**) was a reliable method of dispatching an opposing tank as the side armour was

invariably thinner than that on the glacis or turret front; even better was the rear shot, although this could rarely be obtained.

Figure 6 shows a tank squadron advancing across a series of crest lines using fire and movement by troops. The movement of troops is covered at all times by the hull-down fire of the rest of the squadron. Squadron Headquarters and 4 Troop will not leave the first crest until 1, 2 and 3 Troops have reached the intermediate crest; similarly, the latter will not continue their advance to the third crest until SHQ and 4 Troop have come forward to shoot them in from the intermediate crest. This method, sometimes referred to as movement by bounds, is used in reverse to cover a withdrawal.

Below: Taken from the turret of the troop leader's tank, this photograph illustrates the principles of fire and movement within a three-tank troop. Two tanks are crossing the exposed railway line and will probably halt at the shallow crest in the middle distance. On the right, the third tank provides cover while they move, positioning itself against the most likely source of trouble, the ruined railway station. The rest of the troop will then cover it in turn as it advances to join them on the next bound. (National Army Museum)

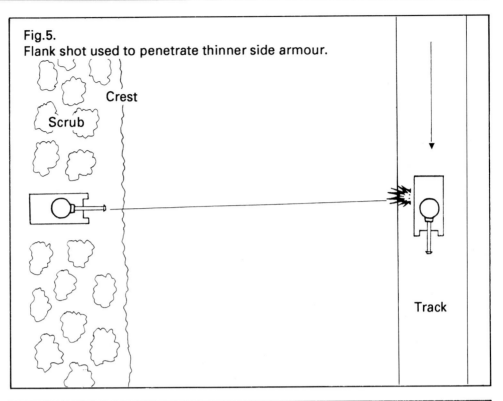

Fig.5.
Flank shot used to penetrate thinner side armour.

Crest

Scrub

Track

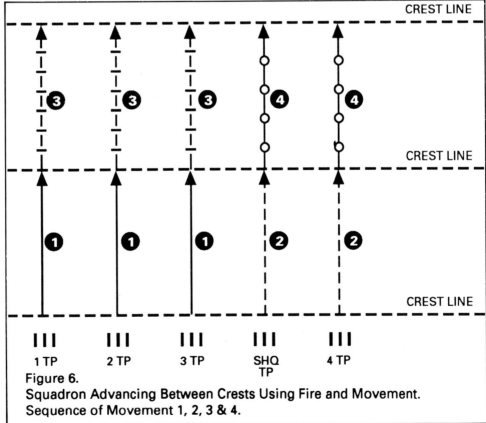

CREST LINE

CREST LINE

CREST LINE

1 TP 2 TP 3 TP SHQ 4 TP
                 TP

Figure 6.
Squadron Advancing Between Crests Using Fire and Movement.
Sequence of Movement 1, 2, 3 & 4.

Above: Aspects of the tank battle (1). A photograph taken by the then Major-General Erwin Rommel from his command vehicle showing the armoured spearhead of 7th Panzer Division advancing across the open French landscape during the 1940 campaign in the west. (IWM)

Below: Aspects of the tank battle (2). An area of Russian resistance has been battered by dive-bombers and tanks are moving forward to finish the job, watched by the German infantry unit which has been pinned down. (IWM)

Above: Aspects of the tank battle (3). An astonishing picture showing part of the mêlée near Prokhorovka on 12 July 1943. This, the greatest tank battle in history, was fought between the 700 tanks of Hoth's Fourth Panzer Army and the 850 tanks of Rotmistrov's Fifth Guards Tank Army. (Novosti)

Below: Aspects of the tank battle (4). 79th Armoured Division's specialist teams, including Crabs, AVREs and Crocodiles, crack open the perimeter defences of Le Havre, 10 September 1944. Crocodiles are flaming the forward edge of the wood. (IWM)

THE TACTICAL LEVEL

British infantry/tank attack, Second Battle of Alamein, 1942: The principal task of the infantry divisions of XXX Corps was to secure gaps in the Axis minebelts through which the armoured divisions of X Corps could be passed to engage and defeat the enemy armour. The minebelts were themselves heavily defended and stiff resistance was expected from the enemy infantry; likewise, the Axis armoured formations, deployed just behind the front, would inevitably counter-attack and attempt to eliminate any penetration. XXX Corps infantry were therefore supported by the 200 Valentines of 23 Armoured Brigade (8, 40, 46 and 50 RTR), which carried out exhaustive training with them during the weeks prior to the battle. In an attempt to reduce casualties almost all attacks were carried out at night. The assault itself was led by the infantry with the tanks following close behind, each arm dealing with the other's problems as they arose. The idea was that the tanks should provide the

closest support possible at first light and break up the enemy's armoured counter-attack when it came in. They would then remain on the captured objective until the infantry could bring forward and emplace their own 6pdr anti-tank guns. Once the position had been consolidated they would withdraw and replenish for the next night's operation.

Figure 7(a) shows the start of such an operation. The attack is to be delivered by an infantry battalion with a Valentine squadron in support. The time is 0400 and the objective is under artillery fire. A gap in the minebelt has been cleared by sappers and, after linking up with their tank troops, the rifle companies are moving through this with battalion and squadron headquarters in close proximity. To avoid churning up the going for wheeled vehicles, the tanks stick to their own lane and move in line ahead.

In Figure 7(b) the infantry and tanks have deployed beyond the minebelt and the assault is going in on a two-company frontage. 'B' Company have sustained casualties from a machine-gun post. This has been destroyed by 2 Troop, although in the process the latter have lost a tank to a

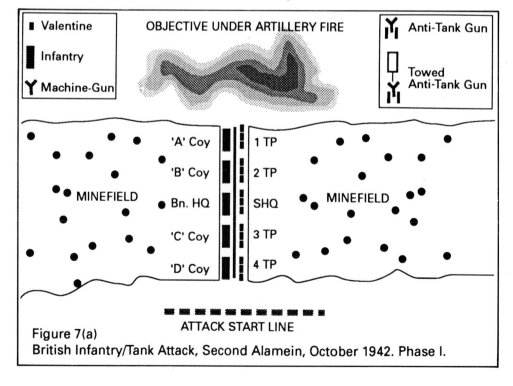

Figure 7(a)
British Infantry/Tank Attack, Second Alamein, October 1942. Phase I.

concealed anti-tank gun, which is in turn stalked and destroyed by the remainder of 'B' Company. The time is now 0430.

Figure 7(c). By 0545 the captured ridge has been consolidated for all-round defence and the tanks have taken up hull-down positions among the infantry. At first light an enemy counter-attack is beaten off by the Valentines and artillery fire controlled by the latter's forward observation officer (FOO). The battalion's anti-tank guns are emerging from the minefield gap and will soon be dug in, enabling the tanks to withdraw.

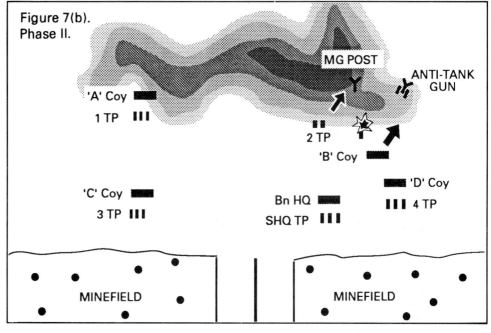

Figure 7(b). Phase II.

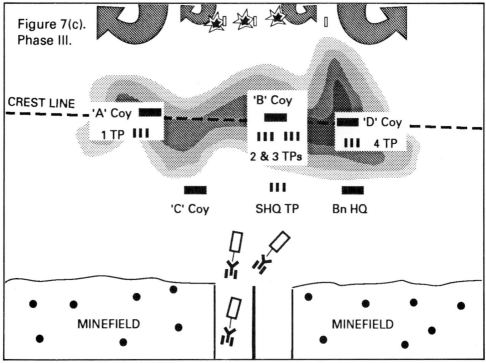

Figure 7(c). Phase III.

Above: Lees support an infantry attack on a Burmese village. (IWM)

Left: Gurkha infantry provide a close escort for a 7th Light Cavalry Stuart, Burma 1945. (IWM)

Top right: Reconnaissance Troop of the 3rd Scots Guards (6 Guards Tank Brigade), equipped with M5A1 Stuarts, leads the regiment forward during the Reichswald battle, February 1945. (IWM)

Right: A Matilda crew forages in the wreck of a Stuka downed inside the Tobruk perimeter. (IWM)

Integrated all-arms attack, Italy, 1945: The Italian landscape, with its successive ridgelines separated by rivers, and vineyards which curtailed tank crew's lateral vision, was ideal defensive country which posed serious problems for an attacker. The answer to these lay in recognizing the need for interdependence between arms and this resulted in an apparently complex but extremely efficient interlock between infantry, armour, artillery and assault engineers. The example below illustrates the working of the technique during the later stages of the campaign.

Figure 8(a) illustrates the opening phase of the battle. The Germans hold Hill **A** in company strength and have forward outposts in the farm **B** and the vineyard **C**. They have the immediate support of a troop of tank destroyers and several dug-in anti-tank guns, as well as artillery on call. Allied troops consist of an infantry battalion with Kangaroo APCs for two companies, a Churchill tank squadron with, under command, one troop of M10 tank destroyers, one troop of Crab flails, one troop of Crocodile flame-throwers, one bridgelayer, one fascine-carrying AVRE, and artillery on call. Patrol activity has revealed that: the river is fordable by infantry but its banks are steep and constitute a tank obstacle; the bridge **D** has been blown and its approaches are mined; the culvert **E** has also been blown and the crater is a tank obstacle.

The task of the Allied commander is to capture Hill **A** and he plans his attack in three phases: I, the river crossing and the capture of the vineyard lying on the left flank of his centre-line; II, the capture of the farm; III, the main assault.

Phase I. Under covering fire provided by the artillery, tanks and M10s (which have the specific task of engaging the enemy's armour, should it appear), the Crabs flail the bridge approach and the bridgelayer puts in its bridge. Screened by smoke shells, the tank squadron's 1 Troop and the Crocodiles cross the bridge while the infantry battalion's 'A' Company ford the river to the north. While the gun tanks provide covering fire the Crocodiles flame the forward edge of the vineyard. It is probable that the enemy outposts are armed with *Panzerfausts* and for this reason 'A' company fights its way through the vineyard ahead of the tanks.

Phase II **(Figure 8(b))**. The tank squadron's 2 Troop cross the bridge while 'B' Company fords the river to the south. With direct fire support from 1 Troop and 'A' Company in the vineyard, 2 Troop and 'B' Company advance on the farm with the

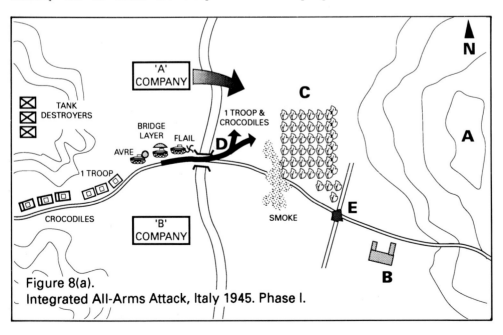

Figure 8(a).
Integrated All-Arms Attack, Italy 1945. Phase I.

tanks leading as far as its outbuildings and the infantry beyond. As the assault goes in the artillery FOO lifts the concentrations which have been falling on the farm. Once the farm has fallen the AVRE drives forward and drops its fascine into the culvert.

Phase III **(Figure 8(c))**. The start-line for the assault on Hill A is between the vineyard and the farm. Both flanks are now secure and the infantry battalion commander calls up his 'C' and 'D' Companies, who move straight down the road in their APCs, together with the tank squadron's SHQ, 3 and 4 Troops. The FOO calls down concentrations on the objective. The assault goes in with the tanks leading and the infantry dismounted. When the hill has been taken the specialized armour is released, but the tanks remain with the infantry on the objective until the latter's anti-tank guns can be emplaced.

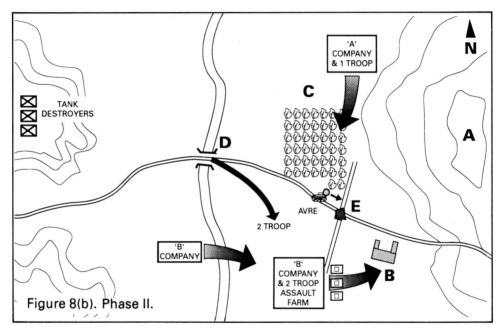

Figure 8(b). Phase II.

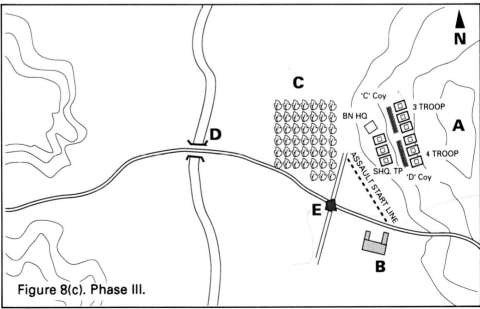

Figure 8(c). Phase III.

Mobile defence by panzer division against Soviet penetration, 1943–4: The Eastern Front's most notable exponent of armoured warfare at the tactical and operative levels was Major-General Hermann Balck, who commanded 11th Panzer Division, XLVIII Panzer Corps and Fourth Panzer Army in succession before moving to the Western Front in 1944. **Figure 9(a)** shows the method he employed to recapture the village of Manutchskaya, twenty miles from Rostov, on 25 January 1943. The Russians had dug in their tanks in the southern half of the village, where they were difficult to spot, and to flush them out Balck mounted a feint attack under cover of a smoke-screen against their northern perimeter, using his armoured reconnaissance battalion and panzergrenadier halftracks. As soon as the Russian tanks broke cover to deal with this the divisional artillery regiment, less one battery which continued to fire smoke-shells to mask the diversion, fired concentrations against the selected break-in point on the southern edge of the perimeter. Balck's panzer regiment burst through the gap and destroyed their unsuspecting opponents among the houses. The remaining Russians

took to their heels but were cut down by the panzergrenadiers. 11th Panzer Division sustained the loss of one killed and fourteen wounded; Russian casualties were in excess of 500 and twenty of their tanks were destroyed.

When faced with a Russian attack, the nature and timing of which could generally be predicted, the Germans would often leave their front line to be held by a chain of warning outposts and withdraw several miles to establish a PaK–Front with their panzergrenadier and tank destroyer units. This meant not only that most of the enemy's artillery preparation was wasted on empty space, but also that his carefully prepared timetable was thrown out of gear. When the Russians eventually closed up to the new position, the German artillery would concentrate on separating the tanks from their infantry, a comparatively easy task in view of the Soviet Army's lack of APCs. At this point the division's panzer regiment would launch a concentrated, and frequently decisive, counter-attack into the Russian flank or rear. Balck was a firm believer in night marches which would place him in a position to strike into the rear of the enemy when they were making their

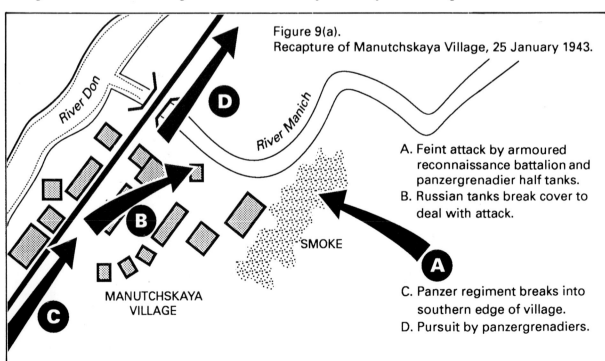

Figure 9(a).
Recapture of Manutchskaya Village, 25 January 1943.

River Don

River Manich

SMOKE

MANUTCHSKAYA
VILLAGE

A. Feint attack by armoured reconnaissance battalion and panzergrenadier half tanks.
B. Russian tanks break cover to deal with attack.
C. Panzer regiment breaks into southern edge of village.
D. Pursuit by panzergrenadiers.

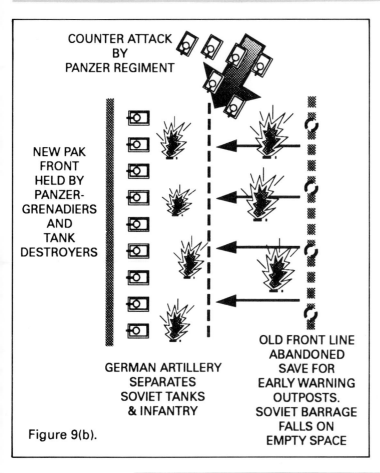

COUNTER ATTACK
BY
PANZER REGIMENT

NEW PAK
FRONT
HELD BY
PANZER-
GRENADIERS
AND
TANK
DESTROYERS

GERMAN ARTILLERY
SEPARATES
SOVIET TANKS
& INFANTRY

OLD FRONT LINE
ABANDONED
SAVE FOR
EARLY WARNING
OUTPOSTS.
SOVIET BARRAGE
FALLS ON
EMPTY SPACE

Figure 9(b).

own attack at first light; this was extremely tiring, especially if carried out on several consecutive nights, but had the dual advantages of simultaneously reducing casualties and achieving complete surprise. In one such counter-attack his panzer regiment destroyed 65 Soviet tanks without loss, the Russians being under the impression that it was their own second wave. The technique is illustrated by **Figure 9(b).**

79th Armoured Division Assault Engineer techniques, D-Day, June 1944. A representative sector of the Normandy coastline is shown in **Figure 10(a).** Two areas of dunes which are impassable to armour are linked by a sea wall. The beach itself is mined and is covered by cross-fire from two bunkers. Inland is a continuous anti-tank ditch covered by fire from a villa which has been converted to a strongpoint. The assault has been timed to coincide with half-tide, which will expose most of the submerged beach obstacles. DD Shermans have just touched down ahead of the infantry landing craft and both tanks and infantry are engaged in suppressing the fire from the bunkers.

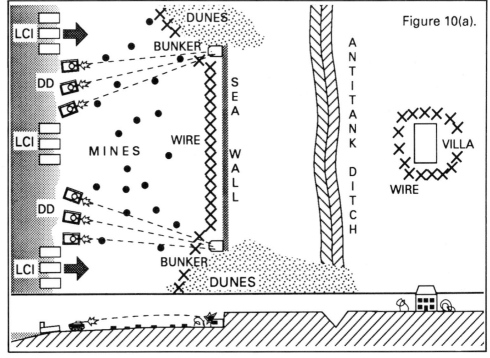

Figure 10(a).

LCI

DD

LCI

MINES

WIRE

DD

LCI

BUNKER

BUNKER

DUNES

DUNES

SEA WALL

ANTITANK DITCH

VILLA

WIRE

In **Figure 10(b)** the LSTs carrying the assault engineer teams have beached successfully. A troop of Sherman Crabs has flailed a path through the mines to the sea wall, then turned aside to permit the passage of AVREs, one of which lays a small box-girder bridge against the top of the wall, forming a ramp. Two more AVREs climb the ramp and drops fascines into the anti-tank ditch; this attracts fire from the fortified villa, which the AVREs batter into submission with their petard mortars. The bunkers covering the shore have now been neutralized and the infantry, supported by DDs, advance through the breach to consolidate the beach-head perimeter. As more troops and equipment land engineers create additional exits from the beach by flailing mine-free lanes, bulldozing routes through the dunes and blowing down sections of the sea wall to create further ramps.

Left: The Grant's roomy interior made it particularly suitable as an armoured command vehicle (ACV). In this version, belonging to HQ 6th South African Armoured Division, the original 37mm has been stripped from the turret and replaced by a much larger dummy. (SANMMHI)

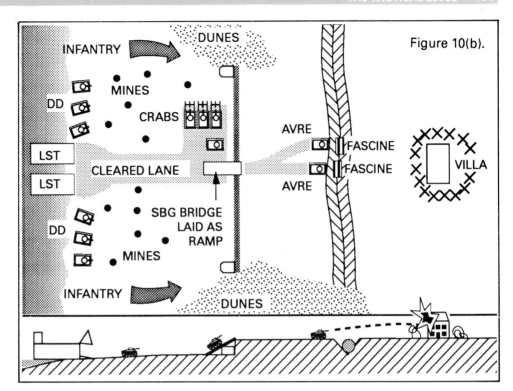

Figure 10(b).

DUNES

INFANTRY

MINES

DD

CRABS

AVRE

FASCINE

FASCINE

VILLA

LST

AVRE

LST

CLEARED LANE

SBG BRIDGE
LAID AS
RAMP

DD

MINES

INFANTRY

DUNES

Below: Sherman dozer manned by an RTR crew filling in a cratered road on II Polish Corps's axis, Italy, 1945. (Sikorski Museum)

THE OPERATIVE LEVEL

Breakthrough by panzer division/corps, 1939–42: The panzer division was a balanced formation designed for offensive use and relied upon its ability to generate intense violence on a comparatively narrow sector, not more than 5,000 yards wide, to create a breach in the enemy's front. The division's order of march would be influenced by the resistance and terrain it expected to meet, but it was always led by its tank element. During the approach march the tanks might be concentrated in a *keil* (wedge) but for the assault itself they would deploy into two consecutive *Treffen* (clubs) or two parallel *Flügel* (wings), each of which was responsible for suppressing a

specific aspect of the defence. Whatever formation was adopted the front ranks would consist of Pz Kpfw IIIs, closely supported by Pz Kpfw IVs ready to engage the enemy's anti-tank guns with their howitzers, while the light Pz Kpfw Is and IIs were deployed to the flanks and rear. The enemy front would be engaged by the divisional artillery, possibly supplemented by that of other formations, and subjected to heavy dive-bombing attacks by the Luftwaffe, all of which would combine to erode the will of the defence. Generally, the sheer speed and weight of the attack would serve to carry it right through the defended zone **(Figure 11(a))**.

Once the breakthrough had been effected the tanks would accelerate towards their strategic objective, avoiding areas of resistance whenever possible. At

Above: Stuart M5A1 of the US 14th Armored Division seriously damaged as a result of a German bomb exploding a case of mines lying near the tank. The final half-shaft, the drive sprocket and additional sandbag protection have all been ripped off. (USAMHI)

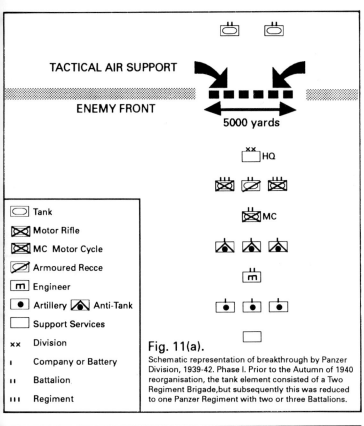

TACTICAL AIR SUPPORT

ENEMY FRONT

5000 yards

Tank
Motor Rifle
MC Motor Cycle
Armoured Recce
Engineer
Artillery   Anti-Tank
Support Services
xx   Division
ı   Company or Battery
ıı   Battalion
ııı   Regiment

Fig. 11(a).
Schematic representation of breakthrough by Panzer Division, 1939-42. Phase I. Prior to the Autumn of 1940 reorganisation, the tank element consisted of a Two Regiment Brigade, but subsequently this was reduced to one Panzer Regiment with two or three Battalions.

Fig. 11(b).
Schematic representation of breakthrough by Panzer Division, 1939-42. Phase II.

1. Armoured Recce Battalion has moved into the lead.

2. Panzer regiment has resumed wedge formation on completion of breakthrough phase.

3. Shoulders of penetration are held by Motor Rifle Battalions reinforced with anti-tank barriers. These units will resume advanced when relieved by follow-up troops.

ENEMY FRONT

this point, however, the armoured reconnaissance battalion would go into the lead, operating several miles ahead of the advance and sending back a flow of information to the divisional commander. In the wake of the tanks would come the motor rifle battalions, which would hold the shoulders of the penetration until relieved and deal with isolated pockets of resistance along the divisional centre-line; the motorized artillery batteries, ready to support tanks or riflemen as the situation demanded; the anti-tank gunners, capable of deploying rapidly into PaK-Fronts with which to beat off an armoured counter-attack; the engineer battalion with its bridging skills; and the division's supply, maintenance, recovery and replenishment service units **(Figure 11(b))**.

The German Army deployed its armoured formations in the offensive at the operative rather than the tactical level and formed panzer corps consisting of two or more panzer divisions; two or more panzer corps constituted a panzer group, the title of which was later changed to panzer army. It was, therefore, unusual for a panzer division to undertake in isolation the sort of operation described above. Normally, the divisions of a panzer corps launched their attack simultaneously within a few miles of one another, tearing a gap in the enemy line which, more often that not, proved impossible to close.

Breakthrough by a Soviet tank army, Eastern Front, 1944: In the autumn of 1944 the Soviet tank corps contained three tank brigades of 65 tanks each; a motor rifle regiment; a light self-propelled artillery regiment with SU-76s; an assault gun/tank destroyer regiment with SU-85s and SU-122s; a light artillery regiment with towed guns; mortar, motor-cycle, engineer and signals battalions; and corps service units. Despite its title, the tank corps was only marginally stronger than a well-equipped German panzer division. Two tank corps constituted a tank army, which might be augmented by a mechanized corps, in which the proportion of tanks to motor rifle troops was reversed. The commander of a tank army also possessed additional artillery, motor-cycle and engineering assets which he could apply where they were needed.

By now the Soviet Army was able to deploy up to 85 tanks and 250 guns per kilometre of front for its offensives, giving an overwhelming superiority of 6/8:1 in tanks and artillery. It was still deficient in radio equipment, but its command and control procedure was a little more flexible in that staff officers familiar with the overall plan were present at every major command level and were authorized to sanction local variations. By way of contrast, Hitler's orders to hold ground regardless of cost had removed much of the German Army's flexibility at the strategic and operative levels.

Figure 12(a) shows the first phase of the tank army's offensive. Like the attack of the panzer division described above, the object is to obtain a breakthrough by generating intense violence on a comparatively narrow sector. The assault is being delivered by the leading tank corps, supported by the corps and army artillery as well as tactical air strikes. The tank brigades are attacking in successive echelons, followed by the motor rifle troops who will clean out the position, shot in by the direct gunfire support of assault gun and tank destroyer units.

Once the breakthrough is a fact the second tank corps will pass through and make straight for its objective, as shown in **Figure 12(b).** The army commander will have placed additional reconnaissance, artillery and engineer units at its disposal. The corps is moving in pre-formed parallel columns which are ready to deploy if the need arises. The real interest, however, lies in the corps advance guard, known as the forward detachment, which consists of a tank brigade, a motor rifle battalion, a self-propelled artillery battalion and an engineer company. The function of this, the precursor of the modern Soviet operational manoeuvre group, was to seize ground of critical importance, bridges, road and rail junctions, which would be needed to maintain the momentum of the advance. On average, during any 24-hour period of an offensive a Soviet tank army would expect to cover approximately ten miles.

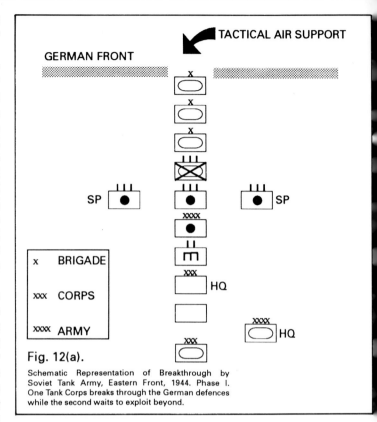

Fig. 12(a).
Schematic Representation of Breakthrough by Soviet Tank Army, Eastern Front, 1944. Phase I. One Tank Corps breaks through the German defences while the second waits to exploit beyond.

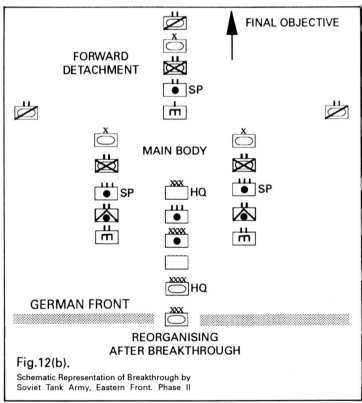

Fig.12(b).
Schematic Representation of Breakthrough by Soviet Tank Army, Eastern Front. Phase II

4. Summary

During the period 1939–1942 the tank dominated the battlefield in much the same way as had the machine-gun and concentrated artillery fire during the First World War. This dominance extended not only to the battlefields of Poland, western Europe, the Soviet Union and North Africa, but also to the Far East, where the Japanese employed a comparatively small number of badly designed tanks to demoralize and inflict a crushing defeat on the tankless British army in Malaya. The reasons why the tank was able to achieve such a commanding supremacy during this period are not hard to find. First, in September 1939 few men had personal experience of being attacked by tanks, which they believed to be invulnerable, unstoppable and terribly dangerous. This arose in part from the fact that during the 1930s less attention was paid to the design of anti-tank weapons than that of tanks, with the result that the former were a half-generation behind and only capable of performing their task in the most favourable circumstances, and in part from the declaration by general staffs that certain geographical features were 'tank-proof' when they were nothing of the kind. In this context the Poles relied vainly on their frontier forests and marshes in 1939, and the French on the rolling woodland of the Ardennes in 1940. Secondly, the complete nature of the tank's victories during the early war years seemed to underline its invincibility, although subsequent analysis would in every case confirm that those victories were obtained over armies that were either under-equipped to meet the threat, or seriously flawed at the command level, in their doctrine or their training. Only the German armoured corps entered the war with a clearly established doctrine which made use of armoured formations at the operative

level to obtain strategic objectives, and because of this and sustained tactical air support it won easy victories over the Poles in 1939, the Western Allies in 1940 and the Russians in 1941–2. The small but well-led British army in Egypt reached similar conclusions and by February 1941 had disposed of its impressively more numerous Italian opponents, although it then lapsed into a period of unorthodoxy which would cost it dear.

By the end of 1942 the effects of the gun/armour spiral were clearly apparent as tanks with more powerful guns and thicker armour began reaching the battlefield. On the other hand, anti-tank gun design had caught up, mobile tank destroyers were already in service, and the arrival of shaped-charge weapon systems meant that the infantry were no longer at the mercy of tanks at close quarters. Likewise, the nature of what has become known as the *Blitzkrieg* technique was now fully understood and it was recognized that the antidote lay in comparable mobility. The tank, once capable of inducing paralysing terror, was vulnerable to a variety of weapon systems and, although it still generated sincere respect, for the second half of the war it performed best as part of an integrated all-arms team capable of providing mutual support. From 1944 onwards wide-ranging operations by armoured formations were only possible after the enemy army had been brought to the point of disintegration, whereas formerly they had themselves been responsible for bringing about its destruction.

This was less immediately apparent on the Eastern Front, where the Soviet Army deployed overwhelming strength and the German response was complicated by Hitler's irrational orders to hold ground at any price, but in Italy and Normandy the pattern was emphasized by terrain that favoured the defence. In the latter case the German armies in the west were bled white by attrition before they were encircled and destroyed, enabling the Allies to sweep across France and Belgium until forced to halt by lengthening supply lines. Once the Rhine was crossed the following year, the German Army, hopelessly fragmented, lacked the means to halt similar drives across its homeland. Conversely, the great German counter-attack through the Ardennes, now known as The Battle of the Bulge, was brought to a standstill partly because the Allies quickly identified Antwerp as its objective and reacted accordingly by deploying formations in its path, partly because, in sharp contrast to 1940, the troops engaged were no longer intimidated by armour, and partly because the panzer divisions were critically short of fuel.

The majority of armies had entered the war with three categories of tank: light, medium or cruiser, and infantry or heavy. In 1945 these categories still existed, although their value as fighting vehicles had risen beyond recognition. The light and heavy classes remained in service for a number of years subsequently, and indeed the former has never entirely disappeared, but the technical advances achieved during the years of the gun/armour spiral, especially the fitting of extremely powerful weapons to the Tigers, the Soviet IS series and the British Centurion, which reached units in Germany just too late to fire its gun in anger, led in post-war years to the merging of the medium and heavy classes into what Field Marshal Montgomery described as the Capital Tank, capable of undertaking any battlefield role, now known universally as the Main Battle Tank (MBT). Since then, in addition to balancing the equation between firepower, protection and mobility, tank designers have been required to install main armament stabilizers, night vision devices, range-finders, fire control computers, navigational aids and overpressure systems as a defence against the possible use of nuclear biological and chemical (NBC) weapons.

Once the MBT was introduced the range at which tank battles were fought opened dramatically, and one consequence of this was the demise of the big-gun tank destroyer, which could no longer offer any improvement on the performance of the tank's main armament. In AFV design, however, offensive innovation is invariably followed by a defensive reaction. When shaped-charge ammunition, capable of penetrating the thickest conventional armour, became available for tank guns, an antidote was produced in the form of a ceramic layer within the main armour which was capable of absorbing the heat of the ultra-high temperature jet before it could reach the vehicle's interior. The shaped-charge round therefore became ineffective against this type of armour and various means have been developed to combat this. Among these is a reversion to kinetic as opposed to chemical energy and for this reason some serious thought has been given to the reintroduction of the big-gun tank destroyer after an absence of almost forty years.

Since 1945 the fortunes of the armoured car have declined somewhat, although it has still had a part to play in counter-insurgency operations during the former colonial powers' withdrawal from empire. On the other hand, the APC has become an essential element in the land battle and now mounts a more powerful armament than did the light tank of 1939. It was recognized in post-war Western armies that the M3 halftrack was not only under-protected for the modern battlefield, but also that as the mobility of tanks increased it would be unable to keep pace with them. Simultaneously, it was accepted that the Kangaroo, while sufficiently mobile, provided too heavy, complex and expensive a solution. The answer therefore lay in producing purpose-built fully tracked APCs that were lighter and more easily maintained than the Kangaroo, yet provided their occupants with overall protection. Having reached this point it was inevitable that APCs would be armed to the point at which they could at the least defeat their own kind. Wheeled APCs were also produced for the counter-insurgency role. In the Soviet Army the adoption of the APC was less of an evolutionary process. Post-war analysis of the Eastern Front battles of 1943–5 confirmed that a major contributory factor in the horrific casualties sustained was the lack of an APC. The concept was therefore embraced with the zeal of the converted, and a wide variety of designs, both wheeled and tracked, were mass-produced before the present generation was accepted.

Likewise, the comparatively simple self-propelled artillery weapons of the Second World War have evolved in terms of armament, protection, mobility and general sophistication, although, with one or two exceptions, the assault gun has gone the way of the tank destroyer. Similar advances have been made in the field of assault engineering, an area in which the Soviet Army is particularly strong, making no bones of the fact that having had its homeland devastated and lost twenty million of its people during the Great Patriotic War, it intends fighting its next war on enemy territory.

Equal progress has been made in the field of anti-tank weapons, so that AFVs are now at greater risk than at any time in their history. Many of these weapon systems are simply evolutionary developments, but others, like the anti-tank guided weapon (ATGW), the tank-hunting helicopter and sensor-guided self-forging warheads which, released as sub-munitions from an artillery-fired carrier shell, penetrate the tank's thinner top surfaces, are extremely dangerous introductions which had no precise wartime equivalent.

In the light of so much technical progress it might be wondered whether the lessons provided by the tank warfare of 1939–45 have any relevance today. The pace at which operations are conducted has been accelerated sharply since 1945, and advances in weapon technology have ensured that in any major war equipment is destroyed on an immense scale, as was evidenced by the Arab/Israeli War of 1973. On the other hand, despite this sophistication, the essential nature of the battle remains substantially the same. The minor tactics and the inter-arms battledrills practised today would be quite intelligible to the veteran of the Second World War, whatever the complexity of the equipment. Equally, at the higher levels, the handling of major armoured formations during the period 1943–5 still exercises some influence on the outlook and planning of both Warsaw Pact and NATO senior officers. This was a period in which the Soviet Army takes great pride, its war academy students being thoroughly grounded in the techniques employed because, suitably adapted, these form the foundation of its concept of offensive warfare. Similarly, contemporary German techniques on the Eastern Front, especially such crushing counter-attacks as that delivered by von Manstein's Army Group South into the flanks of the advancing South West and Voronezh Fronts in February 1943, are studied with great interest in the West. Since 1945 numerous conflicts of varying intensity have tended to confirm that the principles of mechanized warfare established during the war are still fundamentally valid. Today, the commanders of armoured formations have a mass of accumulated experience at their disposal; those of 1939 had only unproven and frequently disputed theories upon which to base their decisions, and equally unproven vehicles with which to implement them, and therein lies the measure of their achievement.

Bibliography

Chamberlain, P., and Ellis, C. *British and American Tanks of World War II*. Arms & Armour Press, 1969

Crow, Duncan. *British and Commonwealth Armoured Formations 1919–1946*. Profile, 1971

Duncan, Nigel. *79th Armoured Division – Hobo's Funnies*. Profile, 1972

Forty, George. *United States Tanks of World War II*. Blandford, 1983

Grove, Eric. *Russian Armour 1941–1943*. Almark, 1977

Macksey, Kenneth. *Tank Tactics 1939–1945*. Almark, 1976

— and Batchelor, John. *Tank*. Macdonald, 1970

Messenger, Charles. *The Art of Blitzkrieg*. Ian Allan, 1976

Ogorkiewicz, Richard M. *Armoured Forces*. Arms & Armour Press, 1970

— *Design and Development of Fighting Vehicles*. Macdonald, 1968

Orgill, Douglas. *T-34 – Russian Armour*. Macdonald, 1970

Perrett, Bryan. *A History of Blitzkrieg*. Robert Hale, 1983

— *Knights of the Black Cross – Hitler's Panzerwaffe and Its Leaders*. Robert Hale, 1986

— *Tank Tracks to Rangoon*. Robert Hale, 1978

Senger und Etterlin, F. M. von. *German Tanks of World War II*. Arms & Armour Press, 1969

— *Kampfpanzer 1916–1966*, J. F. Lehmanns Verlag, 1966

Simpkin, Richard E. *Mechanized Infantry*. Brasseys, 1980

White, B. T. *British Tanks and Fighting Vehicles 1914–1945*. Ian Allan, 1970

Vanguard Series (Osprey): *Allied Tank Destroyers*; *Armour of the Pacific War*; *British Tanks in North Africa 1940–42*; *The Churchill Tank*; *German Armoured Cars and Reconnaissance Half-Tracks 1939–45*; *German Light Panzers 1932–42*; *The Lee/Grant Tanks in British Service*; *Mechanised Infantry*; *The Panzerkampfwagen III*; *The Panzerkampfwagen IV*; *The PzKw V Panther*; *Polish Armour 1939–45*; *The SdKfz 251 Half-Track*; *The Sherman Tank in British Service 1942–45*; *The Sherman Tank in US and Allied Service*; *Soviet Heavy Tanks*; *The Stuart Light Tank Series*; *Sturmartillerie and Panzerjäger*; *The T-34 Tank*; *The Tiger Tanks*; *US Half-Tracks of World War II*

Tanks Illustrated Series (Arms & Armour Press): *Allied Tanks, Italy*; *Allied Tanks, North Africa*